The Life of Fisher
MS. HARLEIAN 6382

Early English Text Society.
Extra Series, No. CXVII.

The Life of Fisher

TRANSCRIBED FROM MS. HARLEIAN 6382

BY

THE REV. RONALD BAYNE, M.A.

SUPPLEMENTARY TO THE ENGLISH WORKS OF JOHN FISHER,
FIRST COLLECTED BY JOHN E. B. MAYOR,
EXTRA SERIES XXVII.

LONDON:
PUBLISHED FOR THE EARLY ENGLISH TEXT SOCIETY
BY HUMPHREY MILFORD, OXFORD UNIVERSITY PRESS,
AMEN CORNER, E.C. 4.

OXFORD

UNIVERSITY PRESS

Great Clarendon Street, Oxford OX2 6DP
United Kingdom

Oxford University Press is a department of the University of Oxford.
It furthers the University's objective of excellence in research, scholarship,
and education by publishing worldwide. Oxford is a registered trade mark of
Oxford University Press in the UK and in certain other countries

© The Early English Text Society 1921 (for 1915)

The moral rights of the authors have been asserted

Database right Oxford University Press (maker)

First Edition published in 1921 (for 1915)

All rights reserved. No part of this publication may be reproduced,
stored in a retrieval system, or transmitted, in any form or by any means,
without the prior permission in writing of Oxford University Press,
or as expressly permitted by law, or under terms agreed with the appropriate
reprographics rights organization. Enquiries concerning reproduction
outside the scope of the above should be sent to the Rights Department,
Oxford University Press, at the address above

You must not circulate this book in any other form
and you must impose this same condition on any acquirer

Published in the United States of America by Oxford University Press
198 Madison Avenue, New York, NY 10016, United States of America

British Library Cataloguing in Publication Data
Data available

Library of Congress Cataloging in Publication Data
Data available

Extra Series, 117

ISBN 978-0-85-991715-5

PREFATORY NOTE

THE following transcript of *Harleian*, 6382, in the British Museum Library, was made many years ago with the intention of collating it with other manuscripts of the Life of Fisher, ascribed to Richard Hall, and adding it to the Works of Cardinal Fisher published by the Early English Text Society. The project has not advanced beyond the setting up in type of the transcript of *Harleian*, 6382. But the transcript is now printed in the hope that it may be found by students a useful addition to the English and Latin Lives published with full notes and introductory matter by the learned Bollandist Father, Fr. Van Ortroy, in the Analecta Bollandiana.

[*Harleian MS.* 6382. *Brit. Mus. Library.*]

[1] A Treatife contayninge the lyfe and manner of death of that moſt holy prelat and conſtant martyr of chriſt, John Fiſher Biſhop of Rocheſter, and Cardinall of the holy church of Rome.

[1] Fol. 1.

THE LIFE OF FISHER.

[1] In the yere of our Redemption 1459, and in the feaven and thirtieth yere of the moft noble & vertuous prince, Kinge Henry the fixt, this holy father and profound Doctor was borne and chriftned at Beverley, in the province of Yorke, a towne dyftant from London northward, about eight fcore myles, where fometime *the* bleffed and glorious Confeffor, St. John of Beverley, Archbyfhop of Yorke, lived and preached. In his baptifme he was named John, of his godfathers, wh*i*ch name he belyed not, as by the difcourfe of his moft gracious lyfe fhall moft cleerly appeare: His parents were of honeft ftate and condition, and by trade of marchandife left behind them a competent wealth; from whofe honeftie, he, by his finguler vertue and learninge, did nothinge detract, but rather added much more then he could receive of them: for vertue and learninge be things fo excellent of themfelves, that they purchafe commendac[i]ou*n*s, both in him in whom they are refident, and to them alfo of whom he fhall defcende; yea, more then they can geve him.

Robert Fyfher his father, after he had lived many yeres in goo eftimac*i*on and credit, dyed, leavinge behind him this John Fyfher o whom we now fpeake; [2] and Robert, both in their tender age. Their mother Ann, in proceffe of time, marryed againe to one named 'wigl. ,' by whom fhe boare three fonnes, named John, Thomas, and Richard, and one daughter called Elizabeth, which after was profeffed a Nun in Dartford. And yet fhe, lyke a tender mother, was not fo affected to her fecond hufband & children that fhe neglected the firft, but remayninge verie carefull of their good educac*i*on, caufed her two

[1] Fol. 2.   [2] Fol. 2, back.

fonnes John and Robert, begotten of her firft hufbande, to be put to learninge at the expences of fuch goodes as their father had left them; and to that end fhe committed them both to a preift of the Church of Beverley, a Collegiat Church of preiftes richly indowed of auncient time with landes and poffeffions, by whom they were (amonge other children) inftructed and taught the firft letters and rudiments of grammer. But this our John Fifher fo far excelled the reft of his fchoole fellowes in his learninge, that it was evident to fee even then, wherto he tended, and what he was lyke to prove vnto in time to come, betokening no doubt the name of 'fifher,' defcendinge from the father, to be in this his fonne John moft properly veryfied, as in whom it pleafed god to elect a fyfher of men, which he after proved in very deed.

[1] After when he came to more mature and wyfe yeres, his mother and other frendes beinge ftill carefull of his weldoinge, began to confider amonge themfelves for what trade of lyfe he was moft fitt: And after they had perceived in him a great dexteritye and aptnes towards learninge; and had further noted him to be, (as he was indeed) naturally indowed with a fober and deep witt, a perfect and ftedfaft memorie, and a will prompt & forward to learne; they thought amonge themfelves no way fo good as to continewe him at ftudie; and thervpon, by a generall confent, he was fent to the vniverfitie of Cambrige, (diftant from his native foile about eight daies iorney fowthward,) which then flowed in learninge, and was througly frequented and furnifhed with Doctors & fchollers comminge from all parts of England, as of auncient time had bene accuftomed.

This John, beinge nowe come to Cambrige, was there committed to the government of maifter william Melton, a reuerend preift and grave Devine; then maifter of the College called Michaell howfe, and Doctor of Divinitie: vnder whom he fo profited, that in fewe yeres he became fingulerly well learned, as well in humanitie, as in logicke; philofophie and other fciences: not ignorant, but well acquainted, [2] with the greeke and heabrew tonges which were then verie ftraungers in this land. Beinge thus furnifhed and inftructed,

---

[1] Fol. 3.   [2] Fol. 3, back.

he proceeded to the degrees of Schoole, and commenced Bacheler of Artes in the yere of our lord 1488, and maifter of Artes the third yere after: and beinge elected fellowe of that howfe: he was alfo fhortly after chofen Proctor of the vniverfitie: In which fpace accordinge to the auncient lawes and ftatutes of his College, he received the holy orders of preifthood. After which time he fell to more profitable learninge, and, leaving all his former ftudie, betooke himfelf to the high and heavenly philofophie, in which, accordinge to the order of fchollers, he kept his difputacion with great laude and commendacion, fo that in fhort fpace he grew to fuch profoundnes, that he was eafily accounted the flower of all the vniverfitie, and at his dewe time proceeded to the dignitie of Bachelor, and after, Doctor of divinity, which, with no fmall praife he achieved in the yere of Chrift 1502.

[1] Whiles thefe things were thus in doinge, it chanced Doctor Melton (whom we before mentioned) to be preferred to the roome of a Chancellor within the Church of Yorke; wherby the maifters place of Michael howfe in Cambrige became voyd, whervnto the fellowes, falling to election of a new maifter, thought none more fit for all caufes then Doctor Fyfher; and therfore, by a full agreement amonge them, they chofe him maifter in the place of Doctor Melton, fometime his Tutor. Then fell it out that the ould proverbe teacheth: 'Magiftratus arguit virum'; for who was more fit to rule and play the maifter, then he that before was well and quyetly ruled whileft he was a fcholler: which in him was well verefied, for after he had continewed certaine yeres in the government of his College, he fo demeand himfelf in that office, that he became not only a myrror or patron to the reft that governed in their feuerall howfes in the vniverfity, but was alfo for his worthines chofen vice chancellor, which roome he inioyed twife together, and therby ruled the whole vniverfitie to his great commendacion and praife.

At length his name grewe fo famous, that, paffinge the bondes of the vniverfitie, it fpred over all the Realme, in fo much as the noble and vertuous ladie, Margaret, [2] Counteffe of Richmond and Darbie, mother to the wife and fage prince kinge Henrie the viith, hearinge

---

[1] Fol. 4.   [2] Fol. 4, back.

of his great vertue and learninge, ceafed not till fhe had procured him
out of the vniverfitie to her fervice, by meane wherof he refigned the
maifterfhip of Michaell howfe and lefte the vniverfitie for *that* time.
After he had a fpace remayned with this noble ladie, fhe perceived
his vertue and good lyfe farr to exceed the fame that before fhe
heard of him, and thervpon foone after made him her ghoftly father:
wherin after he was a while eftablifhed, he ordered himfelf fo
difcretly, fo temperatly and fo wyfely, that both fhe and all her
familie were governed by his high wifdome and difcretion, wherby
at laft he became greatly reuerenced and beloved, not only of the
vertuous ladie, and all her howfhold, but alfo of the kinge her fonne,
with whom he was in no leffe eftimacion and credit all his lyfe after
then with his Miftres: which appeared well not only in the kings
lyfe time, but alfo after his death, for he left him vpon fpeciall truft
for one of his Executors.

[1] Thus remayninge in fervice with the Counteffe of Richmond, he
thought with himfelf not good to fpend his daies in ydlenes, but
calling to his remembrance, that whofoeuer foweth but litle fhall
reape but litle, gave himfelf wholely to practyce that which he had
now well learned: and fo bent himfelf fully to proceed in works of
mercy. And wheras of himfelf he was not able to accomplifh this
charitable and liberall enterprife for lacke of fubftance to anfwere the
fame, he ftudyed by all the meanes he could to provoke others of
more abilitie to fupplie his wante; amonge whom he forgot not this
worthie Counteffe his Miftrefs who although of her felf fhe was verie
liberall and bountifull to all forts of people, yet no doubt through
his occafion fhe much enlarged the fame, not only in her dayly
almes amonge fuch as were poore, but alfo in redemption of Cap-
tives, reperacion of Bridges, and high waies, rewardes towards poore
maides marriages, and diuers other lyke. But he was not fatiffyed
with this worldly foode, for at his perfwafion fhe erected two notable
and goodly Colleges in Cambrige, out of which have fprange manie
notable and profound learned men to *th*e great profit and comoditie of
the whole Church of Chrifte, [2] wherof the one fhe dedicated to Chrift
our Saviour and called it Chrifte College; largely indowing yt with

---

[1] Fol. 5.   [2] Fol. 5, back.

good landes and poffeffions, for maintaynance of learninge and fcience for euer, and faw yt perfectly in her lyfe time built and finifhed of ftone & brick as it now ftandeth. The other College fhe dedicated to St. John the Evangelift, and gave to the fame poffeffions for lyke intent and purpofe; But for as much as this College of St. John was by him finifhed after her death vpon her goods & poffeffions with fome helpe of his owne, more fhall be declared hereafter.

She alfo vpon his motion ordayned a divinitye Lecture in Cambrige and an other in Oxforde, to be openly read in the fchooles for eafe of fuch as fhould be preachers. To the intent that the darke and hard places of holy fcripture might therby be opened and expounded, and for continewance of them both fhe gave good landes wheron the Readers ftipend fhould be paid for euer.

[1] This good father proceeding thus in deeds of charitie, partly procured by the liberallitie of others, and partly by his owne goods fo farr as his abilitie would permitt, befides his daily preaching to the people with moft carefull dilligence, became at laft greatly loved & reuerenced of all fortes of people, efpecially of the reuerend and fatherly Bifhopps then living in England, amonge whom the moft worthie and grave prelate, Doctor Richard Foxe, Bifhopp of winchefter, then in noe fmall eftimacion and authoritie with king Henrie the feaventh (of whofe Counfell he was) boare towards him a great affection and good will, highly commending him to the kinge alwaies when he fawe convenient time and place; only for the vertuous lyfe and perfect fanctitie he perceived in him.

It happened that about the fame time by the death of Maifter William Barnes, Bifhopp of London, Maifter Richarde Fitzjames, then byfhop of Rochefter, was tranflated from thence to the Sea of London: wherby the bifhopricke of Rochefter became void. Then the kinge (as he to whom the nominacion of the next incumbent by cuftome of the Realme belongeth) began to confider with himfelf where a fitt and worthie paftor might be found; [2] The place was defired of manie and no folicitacion wanted to the kinge, every man fetting forward his frend as affeccion led him: But the kinge of his

[1] Fol. 6.   [2] Fol. 6, back.

owne meere motion, infpired by the holy ghoft, named Doctor Fifher his mothers Chaplaine to *that* Bifhoprick contrarie to the expectacion, as well of them that wifhed the place as of many others : and directing his letters to the Chappeter of the Church, required them to name the nomination for their paftor : whervnto they ftraight waies agreed moft gladly, without any contradiccion or negative voice of any one of them, and fo offered vnto him the place foone after ; But when Doctor Fyfher vnderftood what was done, he vtterly refufed the offer, and would in no wyfe accept fuch a charge. Neuertheles at laft by perfwafion of many of his frendes that declared vnto him the great neceffitie of the Church at that time, and fpecially of his old frend the Bifhop of Winchefter, he accepted the burthen, much againft his will, and fhortly after was confirmed byfhop of Rochefter from the Sea Apoftolick by our holy father Julius the fecond, in the monnth of October, the yere of our redemption 1504, and of his age *anno.* 45.

[1] Now for that the king had thus fodenly preferred this man to the high promocion of a Bifhoprick, being but a Chaplen to the Counteffe his mother, & neuer yet advaunced to any other dignitie in the church before, many thought that it was by the cheefe procurement of his Mi*ſ*tre*ſs* the lady Margaret, and foe diuers would fay to the kinge ; but indeed it was farre otherwife for the king when he heard any man fpeake of yt, would folemnely affirme, and openly proteft that he never promoted him to yt, ether vpon the fuite of his mother or of any other perfon livinge, nether yet (as they call yt) for price or prayer, but only for the pure devotion, perfect fanctitie and great learninge he fawe in him. Of which the kings bountifull liberallitie, he himfelf maketh alfo fome mention in the Statute*s* of St. Johns College in Cambrige, prayfing much the honor of the kinge, at whofe handes he fo frankly and freely received this donation. He maketh alfo reherfall fomwhat therof in his dedicatorie epiftle to Richard, Bifhop of Winchefter, before the booke he wrote againft Oecolampadius, where he nameth *th*e kinge for his cheefeft and beft patron, by the wordes of w*h*ich epiftle he feemeth to conceive much ioy and comforte, [2] that it came to him in that forte.

[1] Fol. 7.   [2] Fol. 7, back.

His wordes be thefe "Habeant alij proventus pinguiores etc." Which may be thus englifhed. "Although" (faith he) "fome others have greater rentes and fatter benefices then I, yet I have in ftedd therof leffe charge and cure of foules, fo that when account fhall be made of both (which vndoubtedly will be verie fhortly) I would not wifh my felf in better ftate of livinge the valewe of one heare,"—which wordes were verie well confirmed by the fequell of his doings: for although he was after at one time offered the Bifhoprick of Lincolne, and at an other time the Bifhoprick of Eelye, at the handes of King Henrie the viij[th], any of them both being a farr greater livinge then Rochefter was, yet would he neuer accept fuch offer in that refpect.

After this great and waightie preferment of a Bifhoprick, there fell alfo vnto him even at the fame time an other promotion, of nether fmall moment nor yet voyd of charge, for the vniverfitie of Cambrig, confidering with themfelues what benefit they had received at his handes, and how much they were bound vnto him for the fame, and doubting left they might feeme forgetfull or ingratefull of his goodnes and [1] good will towards them alreadie fhewed, determined to confider him with all the honor they could, knowinge themfelves nether able to reward him with any riches, nor him (who looked for reward only at gods handes) defirous of worldly wealth: and therfore by a full confent they chofe him their high Chauncellor, which is the greateft magiftrate that they can make, for amonge them he beareth the authoritie and iurifdiccion of an Archbifhop, and is alfo their high iudge in all temperall caufes.

My lord of Rochefter having now receiued this dignity was not vnmindfull of that belonged to the fame, for knowing indeed what a precious thing learninge is in all regimentes, and what they were ouer whom this his authoritie was to be vfed, he did not fo much efteeme the dignitie which it contayned, as he well wayed the care thervnto annexed. But before we declare any thing of his doings in the vniverfitie, I think it beft to returne to his paftorall cure at Rochefter, & open vnto you fomwhat of his proceeding there.

Beinge not ignorant of what a burdenous & terrible yoke he had

[1] Fol. 8.

taken vpon him by accepting the care of a Bifhoprick, he determined now to beftowe all his wittes and fenfes how to play the part [1] of a trew byfhop; And firft becaufe there is fmall hope of health in the members of that body where the head is ficke, he began his vifitacion at his head Church of Rochefter, calling before him the Pryor and monkes, exhorting them to obedience, chaftitie, and trewe obfervacion of their monafticall vowes, and where any falte was tryed he caufed it to be amended; After that he carefully vifited the reft of the parifhe Churches within his Dioceffe in his owne perfon: and fequeftring all fuch as he found vnworthie to occupye that high function, he placed other fitter in their roomes. And all fuch as were accufed of any crime, he put to their purgation, not fparing the punifhment of Simonie and Herefie, with other crymes and abufes: And by the way he omitted nether preaching to the people, nor confirming of children, nor releeving of needie and indigent perfons. Soe that by all meanes he obferved a dewe comlines in the howfe of god, which being done, he returned him to his Cathedrall Church: and there to recount how vertuoufly, to the godly example of others, he ordered his life, it fhould be tedious, were it not that the labour in reading may eafily be recompenfed with the great profitt which the ftudious of vertue may reape of fo fruitefull [2] examples; for there is nothing noted in him which may not greatly ferve to the inftruccion of the vnlearned, & for godly immitacion of thofe which otherwife be not ignorant.

It is an old faying and trewe: 'well hath he liued that well hath lurked.' Truly of all the Bifhopps that we have knowne or heard of in our daies, it may beft be faid, that this Bifhopp hath well lived, and well and fecretly lurked: for who hath at any time feene him ydle walke or wander abroad? when did he frequent the Courtes and howfes of Princes and noble men to the entent (as the ould proverbe fayth) to fee and be feene? where did he vfe to banquett and feaft? what noble men or others hath he for pleafure invited? what companie hath vfed to refort vnto him for ydle talke or dryving awaie of time? whom hath he excluded from him that in any wife he might profitt? Yf ye will call that man occupyed that is ftill

[1] Fol. 8, back.   [2] Fol. 9.

occupied in worldly bufines, then cannot that be verified in him, for he lived moſt commonly alone, callinge himſelfe to a dayly account of his lyfe, vſing the Church as a Cloyſter, and his ſtudie as a cell. As long as he was in contemplacion he kept aloane, but when action ſhould be vſed, his divine wordes founded full lowde in all mens eares. what ſhould I vſe many words? [1] All paſtors and Curates vſed him for their lanterne, as one of whom they might perfectly learne when to vſe action, and when contemplacion : for in theſe two things did he ſo far excell, that hard it were to find one ſo well practyſed and expert in any one of them aparte, as he was in both of them together.

Conſider the time when Martin Luther, the moſt damnable and wicked Hereticke that ever was, began to ſpringe, and you ſhall not finde a ſtowter champion againſt him in all his time nor ſince, then was this religious Biſhop, for Luther (as I have heard) began to ſowe his wicked and diveliſh doctrine in Germanie the yere of our lord god 1507, at which time my lord of Rocheſter had gouerned the Sea about 12 yeres, not without the greate providence of Almighty god, that even at his firſt comming on land in England, no ſleeping dogge, nor rude nor ignorant ſhepherd might be found, but a vigilant paſtor, a ſinguler cunning and learned Biſhopp, to catch the yonge cubb or foxe at his firſt arivall. O wicked Luther, great is the miſerie and calamitie that thou haſt brought into this Realme of England, and much greater and ſooner had yt bene but for this worthie prelates reſiſtance, [2] yet never couldeſt thou have entred at all, had he not bene taken away by ſuch as thou haddeſt infected with thy pernitious poyſon. But of this Luther more ſhall be ſaid hereafter in place convenient.

We have hitherto declared vnto you his great and painfull dilligence in preachinge the word of god, which cuſtome he vſed not only in his yonger daies, when health ſerved, but alſo even to his extreame age, when many times his wearie and feeble leggs were not able to ſuſtaine his weake body ſtanding, but forced him to have a chaire, and ſo to teach fitting. Now conſidering this his painfull travell in preaching abroade, what time can you thinke was left for

[1] Fol. 9, back.   [2] Fol. 10.

him to pray, or to write. firft do but beholde his works alreadi҉ extant in printe : then confider diuers others that he hidd, and are not yet come to lighte : Then remember what a number of notable bookes by him compiled haue perifhed by the malice of Hereticks, and ye fhall eafily finde, that he was a man of fuch reading and wrytinge, as may feeme to be only occupied therin and nothing els, which no doubt came by the benefitt and goodnes of Almightie god indewing him with fo divine a witt, fo quick invention, and fo retayninge a memorie, wherby he difpofed & vttered his matter with great learning, zeal and gravitie.

[1] Befydes this he neuer omitted fo much as one Collect of his dayly fervice, and that he vfed to fay commonly to himfelf alone, without the helpe of any Chaplen, not in any fuch fpeedie or haftie manner to be at an ende as many will doe, but in moft reverent and devout manner, fo diftinctly and treatable[2] pronouncing everie word, that he feemed a verie devowrer of heavenly food, never fatiate nor filled therwith : In fo much as talking on a time with a Carthufian monke, who much commended his zeale & dilligent paines in compiling his booke againft Luther, He anfwered againe fayinge, that he wifhed that time of wryting had bene fpent in prayer, thinking that praier would have done more good, and was of more merrit. And to help this his devotion, he caufed a great hole to be digged through the wall of his church of Rochefter, wherby he might the more commodioufly have profpect into the Church at maffe & evenfonge times. When him felf fhould fay maffe, as many times he vfed to doe, yf he were not letted by fome urgent and great caufe, ye might then perceive in him fuch erneft devotion that many times the teares would fall from his cheeke. And left that [3] the memorie of death might happ to flipp from his minde, he alwaies accuftomed to fett upon one ende of the Altar a dead mans fcull, which was alfo fett before him at his table as he dyned and fupped. And in all his praers and other talke he vfed continewally a fpeciall reuerence and devotion to the name of Jefus. Now to thefe his prayers he adioyned two winges, which were Almes & faftinge, by the helpe wherof they might mount the fpeedier to heaven. To poore fick

[1] Fol. 10, back. [2] treatably. Harleian 6896 7049. [3] Fol. 11.

perfons he was a phifitian, to the lame he was a ftaffe, to poore
widdowes an advocate, to orphanes a Tutor, and to poore travellers
an Hoft. Wherfoeuer he lay ether at Rochefter or els where, his
order was to inquire where any poor ficke folkes lay neere him,
which after he once knewe, he would dilligently vifitt them, and
where he faw any of them lykely to die, he would preach to them,
teaching them the waie to die with fuch godly perfwafions, that for
the moft part, he never departed till the ficke perfon were well
fatiffied and contented with death; many times was his chaunce to
come to fuch poore howfes, as for want of chymneys were verie
fmokie and therby fo noyfome that fcant any men could abide in
them, neuertheles himfelf would there fitt by the ficke patient many
times the fpace of 3 or 4 howres together in the fmoke when none of
his fervantes were able to abyde [1] in the howfe, but were faine
to tarry without till his comminge abroade. And in fome other
poore howfes where ftayres were wantinge, he woulde neuer difdaine
to clymbe by a ladder for fuch a good purpofe. And when he had
geven them fuch ghoftly comfort as he thought expedient for their
foules, he would at his departure leave behind him his charitable
almes, geving charge to his fteward or other officers daily to prepare
meat convenient for them (yf they were poore), and fend it to them.
befids this he gave at his gate to diuers poore people (which were
commonly not fmall number) a dayly almes of money, to fome
2^d, to fome 3^d, fome 4^d, fome 6^d, and fome more, after the rate of
their neceffitie. That being done euery of them was rewarded
lykewife with meate which was dayly brought to the gate. And left
any fraude, parcialitie, or other diforder might ryfe in diftribucion of
the fame, he provided himfelf a place wheruuto immediatly after
dynner he would refort, and there ftand to fee the devifion with his
owne eyes.

Yf any ftraungers came to him he would entertaine them at his
table accordinge to their vocacions with fuch mirth as ftood with the
gravitie of his [2] perfon, whofe talke was alwaies rather of learninge or
contemplacion then of worldly matters: And when he had no
ftraungers, his order was now and then to fitt with his Chaplens,

[1] Fol. 11, back.   [2] Fol. 12.

which were commonly grave & learned men, amonge whom he would put fome great queftion of learninge, not only to provoke them to better confideracion and deep fearch of the hidden myfteries of our religion, but alfo to fpend the time of repaft in fuch talke that might be (as it was in deed) pleafant, profitable, and comfortable to the wayters and ftanders by, and yet was he fo daintie and fpare of time, that he would neuer beftow fully an houre at any meale. His dyet at table was for all fuch as thither reforted plentifull and good, but for himfelf verie meane: for vpon fuch eating daies as were not fafted, although he would for his health vfe a larger dyett then at other times, yet was it with fuch temperance, that commonly he was wount to eate and drinke by waight and meafure. And the moft of his fuftinance was thinn pottage fodden with flefh, eating of the flefh it felf verie fparingly. The ordinarie faftes appointed by the church he kept verie foundly, and to them he ioyned many other perticuler faftes of his owne devotion, as appeared well by his thynne and weake body, whervpon though much flefh was not left, yet would he punifh the verie fkinne and bones vpon his [1] backe. He wore moft comonly a fhirt of heare, and many times he would whipp himfelf in moft fecret wife; when night was come, which commonly bringes reft to all creatures, then would he many times difpatch awaie his fervantes, and fall to his praiers a longe fpace. And after he had ended the fame, he laid him downe vpon a poore hard Cowch of ftrawe and matts, (for other bed he vfed none) provided at Rochefter in his clofett, neere the Cathedrall Church, where he might looke into the Quyer and heare divine fervice; and being laid he never refted above 4 howres at a time, but ftraight waies rofe and ended the reft of his devout prayers. Thus lived he till towardes his later daies, when being more growne into age, which is (as Cicero faith) a ficknes of it felf, he was forced fomwhat to relent of thefe hard and fevere faftes, and the rather for that his body was much weakned with a confumption; wherfore by counfell of his phifitian, and licence of his ghoftly father, he vfed vpon fome fafting dais to comfort himfelf with a litle thynne grewell made for the purpofe.

The care that he had of his familie was not fmall, for although

[1] Fol. 12, back.

his cheefeft burthen confifted in difcharge of his fpirituall function, yet did he not neglect his temperall affaires; wherfore he tooke fuch order in his [1] revenuews, that one part was beftowed vpon reparacion and maintenance of the Church, the fecond vpon the releef of povertie and maintaynance of fchollers, and the third vpon his howfhould expenfes, and buying of bookes, wherof he had great plentie. And left the trooble of worldly bufines might be fome hyndrance to his fpirituall exercife, he vfed the helpe of his brother Robert, a lay man, whom he made his Steward fo longe as his faid brother lived, giving him in charge fo to order his expenfes that by noe meanes he brought him in debte. His fervants vfed not to weare their apparrell after any courtly or wanton manner, but went in garments of a fadd and feemely colour, fome in gownes and fome in Coates as the fafhion then was, whom he alwaies exhorted to frugallitie and thrifte, and in any wife to beware of prodigallitie, and where he marked any of them more geven to good hufbandrie then others, he would many times lend them money, and never afke yt againe, & commonly when yt was offered him, he did forgeve it. Yf any of his howfeholde had committed a falte, as fomtime it happened, he would firft examine the matter himfelf, and finding him faultie, would for the firft time but punifh him with wordes only, but it fhould be done with fuch a seuerritie of countenance and gravitie of fpeech that whofoeuer came once before him was verie vnwilling [2] to come before him againe for any fuch offence. So that by this meanes his howfhould continewed in greate quyetnes and peace; everie man knowinge what belonged to his dutie. Some amonge the reft (as they could gett oportunitie of time) would applie their mind to ftudie and to wrytinge; and thefe above all others he fpecially lyked, and would many times fupport them with his labour, and fomtimes with his money. But where he fawe any of them geven to Idlenes and flouth, he would by no meanes indure them in his howfe, bycaufe out of that fountaine many evills are comonly wont to fpringe; In conclufion his familie was governed with fuch temperance, devotion and learning, that his Pallace for

---

[1] Fol. 13.   [2] Fol. 13. back.

continencie feemed a verie Monafterie; and for learning an vniverfitie.

As he was difcreet in vfing feveritie, when *the* inordinate and too exceffive behavio*ur* of the offender did neceffarily require correction, fo was he comfortable and fweet towards fuch as needed confolac*i*on: wherin truly he had fuch a divine grace that he came to few in their heavines and forrowes whom, ere he left them, he did not much eafe, which amongft the number his old Mi*ftrefs* the lady Margarett [1]did often find at his handes, for at fuch time as fhe was in great hevines for the death of her only fonne that noble prince King Henrie the vij[th]., which happened in the yere of our redemption 1509, She was not fooner adu*er*tifed of the co*m*ming of this holy father to vifitt her, but i*m*mediately fhe found herfelf bettered. And after fhe had talked with him a fpace was for the time well fatiffyed and comforted: for he knewe well (as moft learnedly he declared in a funerall fermon, w*h*ich vpon Sundaie the xth of Maie in the yere before named, he made for the forefaid prince: whofe vertues and noble actes he there co*m*mendeth, to the great example of other fuch princes as he was), That though death be tirrible of all other things, as Ariftotle reporteth, yet feeing we can by noe meanes avoid it, that the beft waie is, to acquaint our felves with it by often thinking and recording of yt, that when it co*m*meth in deed it may feeme leffe ftrange: Even as we fee thofe bandoggs and maftiff*es* that be tyed in chaines: for vnto fuch as doe often vifitt them they be more gentle and eafie, but againft ftraungers that have noe acquaintance or familiaritie with them, they furioufly ryfe and gape to devoure them: which leffon yf we could well learne, we fhould no doubt take death more patiently, when it co*m*meth, both in our felves and others, as doubtles this good lady did, who through the great comfort fhe tooke in this [2] and other his holy exhortac*i*ons (after the funeralls of her fonne the king were ended), began to returne where fhe had be*n*ne, and did then fett her minde wholely to the encreafe of her charitie and almes deedes; which the rather *that* fhe might doe with effect, fhe called vnto her this good byfhopp co*m*mitting vnto him all the charge of this her charitable entent,

[1] Fol. 14.   [2] Fol. 14, back.

wherin he had lately before moved her. I meane for the erection of her foundac*i*ons in Cambrige which above others they thought moſt neceſſarie to be diſpatched, in as much as the care and benefit of *th*e foule is to be *p*referred before the bodie, for at that time hereſies began faſt to ſpringe; therfore with as much convenient ſpeed as might be, my lord ſpeeds himſelf to Cambridge, and there by vertue of his office of high Chaunceller looked verie ſtraitly to *th*e orders and rules of the vniuer*ſ*itie, calling eue*r*y man to his dutie aſwell in the ſchooles for profit of their learninge, as in their Churches and Colleges for dewe keeping and obſerving the ſervice of god, indevoringe himſelf, by all the meanes he could, to reduce *th*e vniuer*ſ*itie to their aunctient rules and ſtatut*es*, which began even then to growe out of frame. And where he ſaw any that with example of obedience and profit in learninge exceeding the reſt, them he would encorrage & advaunce by all the meanes he coulde. Others that he ſawe [1]incline to the contrarie, he would expell, or avoyding of other hurt that might inſewe by their example. Some others that he perceived to loyter being apt to doe better, yf they lifted to put to their wills, he did artificially encorrage and quicken, vſing ſuch meanes, that with verie ſhame he drove them forwards; And many times for the encorragment of the yonge ſort, himſelf would be p*r*eſent at their diſputac*i*ons and reading*es* and in diſputing among them would beſtowe ſometimes many how*r*es together.

And here I cannot omitt to declare vnto you one ſinguler token and example of his great love and charitable mind towards the vniuer*ſ*itie, which happened on a time as he lay at Cambrige occupied in the buſines of his office of Chauncellorſhip, at which time Luther in Saxonie had burſt out with a venemous tonge in rayling & crying againſt holy indulgences, commonly called pardons. It fell out ſo that Pope Leo the xth graunted out a gene*r*all and free pardon (according to the aunciente cuſtome and tradition of the Church) to all chriſtian people contrite and confeſſed, through all provinces of *Chriſt*endome, and ſpecially to all ſuch as with worde and deed withſtoode this new develiſh and pernitious doctrine ſet forth by

[1] Fol. 15.

Luther: which pardon in preſſe of time came into England, and divulged into all partes of the Realme. This godly man then Chauncellor of the vniuerſitie of Cambrige; thinking not good to neglect the [1] benefitt therof, but with hartie defire embracinge the holefome remedie of fuch a gratious medicine, foughte meanes to cure as many therwith as he coulde, that afwell ftudientes of the vniuerfitie as others there, might haue their partes of that heavenly treafure: wherfore he commaunded, that certaine copies of the faid indulgences (which then were in printe) fhould be fett vp in fundrie publique places of the vniuerfitie, wherof one was fixed on the Schoole gate: Now were there at that time in Cambrige, fome of lyke ill fpirit as Luther was in Saxonie, though they were verie fecrett, and in number verie fewe, who as far as they durft went about to deprave the authoritie therof, amonge whom a certaine wretched and pernitious perfon at that time in the vniuerfitie, envyinge the fpirituall profitt of others, readinge on a daie the forefaid indulgence vppon the fchoole gate, began ftraight waie by inftigacion of fome ill fpirit, to excogitate and thinke, how he might both flaunder the authoritie of the Pope, & hinder the benefit of the pardon in the hartes of good people, whervpon fecretly in the night, comming to the fchoole gate where the pardon ftood, he wrote vpon it thefe wordes; "Beatus vir cuius eſt nomen domini ſpes eius, et non refpexit [2] vanitates et infanias falfas (iftas)," wrefting therby the fence of that place of holy fcripture from the trew meaninge by adding to the text this word "iftas" of his owne malicious invention and devife. In the morninge the fchooles beinge fett open, and the fchollers of all fortes reforting thither, according to their wonted manner, many beheld this ftrange fpectacle: and as the good Catholickes were much offended with the wicked kind of abufinge holy fcripture in fo great a matter, fo the contrarie fort began amonge them felves to fmile and fecretly reioyce in approvinge the facte; what fhould I vfe many words? This matter being at laſt brought to the Chauncellers knowledge, he was greatly moved at the deteftable & wicked deede. And thervpon fell immediatly to find out the dooer, firſt by trying the hand wrytinge, and after by other

---

[1] Fol. 15, back.   [2] Fol. 16.

meanes, but all in vaine, for yt could not be found out. At laft in a publick Convocac*i*on called for that purpofe, he opened *the* cafe, and there before them openly detefted *that* abhominable kind of dealinge. And firft he approveth and aloweth *the* Popes pardons accordinge to their worthines, and after expoundeth the trewe fence of that place of fcripture w*h*ich before by that wretched perfon was depraved and wrefted, condemninge him of vanitie and falfhood, that would foe vainly and falfly ufurpe any place of holy fcripture to the fenfuallitie of his owne foolifh and malicious brain. Then he declared what great difpleafure might iuftly infewe, at the handes of Almightie god and the kinge in [1] case this horrible fact fhould be left vnpunifhed. After that what a great difcredit it would be to their whole vniue*r*fitie (being hitherto neue*r* fufpected of any hereticke comm*i*ng out of her) yf now fuch a malefactor fhould efcape and not be inquired of. In conclufion before the whole affemblie there congregate, he moved the Author to repentance, and by confeffion of his falt to afke forgevenes at gods handes, which yf he would do by a certaine day there prefixed vnto him (fo as himfelf might alfo have knowledge therof) he promifed in gods behalf remiffion. But yf on the contrarie part, he would obftinately perfift and continewe in his feacret naughtyneffe, that then fuch remedie fhould proceed againft him as C*h*rift hath ordayned, and his Church hath alwais obferved againft thofe kind of malefactors, who lyke rotten members are by the fenfure of excomu*n*icac*i*on cut of from the body of the Church, and fo deprived of all fuch grace & benefitte*s* as obedient and trewe members to their great comfort do inioy, whiles they continew in their mothers bofome; for the malefactor fo cutt of be he neue*r* fo odd or fecret in his naughtines for a time, yet can he not be hidden from god, who will not fail to lay his hand vpon him when yt fhall be too late for him to repent. After he had fpoken thefe wordes, or the lyke, with great fervitie the convocac*i*on was for that time diffolved, and fo every man departed till the appointed day that *the* excomu*n*icac*i*on fhould be pronounced: when the day was come & *the* affemblie [2] readie, which was no fmall number at fo rare a Cafe, the chauncellor there moved the malefactor the fecond time, to repentance and

[1] Fol. 16, back.   [2] Fol. 17.

confeffion of his offence: but the fpiritt that before fuggefted this wicked attempt into his hart, wold by no meanes fuffer him to hearken to any amendment. Wherfore the Chauncellor feeing the ficknes defperate, and not lyke to be cured in fo obftinate and ftubborne a patient, feared moft the infection of others, and therfore fell to this laft and extreame remedie. And fo caufing a bill of excomunicacion to be written, tooke the fame in his handes and began to reade yt, but after that he had proceeded a fpace in the reading therof, he ftayed, and began againe to confider in his minde the great waight of this greevous fentence, which fo much pearced his hart, that even before them all he could not refraine weepinge. The avditorie feeing that lamentable fight fell lykewife to fuch a compaffion, that afwell the auncient reverend doctors and maifters, as other ftudientes of the yonger fort, perceivinge the milde nature of that holy man fell eftfoones into great weepinge and lamentacion, and fo left of without furder proceeding in the excomunicacion for that time, Neuertheles appointing a third day for that purpofe, againft which time yf he came not in, then to proceed to the end without any further delay. This third day being at laft come, and the Convocacion fully affembled, it was declared by the Chauncellor with a heavie countenance that no tydings [1] could be learned of this ungodly perfon nether of any confeffion or repentance by him made or donne, according to the duty of a Chriftian man, in recompence of fo ill and wicked a fact. Wherfore nowe feeing no other remedie to be found, thought it neceffarie and expedient to proceed: And fo orderinge himfelf after a grave and fevere manner as well in his countenance as other gefture of his bodye he pronounced this tirrible fentence from the beginninge to the endinge, againft this defperat and wicked perfon, but not without weepinge and lamentacion: which ftrooke fuch a fear into the harts of his hearers, when they heard his fearfull & tirrible wordes, that moft of them beinge prefent, efpecially of the yonger fort, looked when the ground fhould have opened and fwallowed him vp prefently before them, as a right reuerrend and worthie prelat once tould me, which then was a yonge man and prefent at all bufines: fuch was the bitternes of his

[1] Fol. 17, back.

wordes, and gravitie of his fentence. But although for that prefent time the minde of this miferable man was fo hardned with obftinat ftubbornnes, that it could by none of thefe meanes be induced to repentance and confeffion of this fo deteftable Acte, but ftill continewed in that wilfull blyndnes, with deepe and clofe diffimulacion for a fpace after: yet did not this holy mans zealous wordes and pittifull teares, fpent in compaffion of the wretched foul altogether perifhe; for not longe after they wrought fo in him that they never [1]went out of his minde, but ingendred fuch remorfe of confcience in his breft, that although meere neceffitie forced him hereafter to forfake the vniuerfitie, and become a fervant to Doctor Goodrich then fuperentendent of Elye, a vehemente Heretick and ill difpofed perfon, yet could he neuer be brought to thinke otherwife, but that he had fore offended almightie god, in contemning him in one of his fo worthie vicars as was this our holy byfhopp, with open deteftacion of this naughtie doinge: Infomuch as when any of his fellowes fervantes or other in that howfe, would ieft at him & put him in remembrance of his former acte (as many times they would) he would euer blame them for fo doinge, reherfing to them this verfe of the pfalmift. Delicta iuuentutis meæ et ignorantias ne memineris domine. This man was named Peter de Valence, by calling a preift, and borne in Normandie, from whence he fledd, and comminge to Cambrige for ftudie remayned there till this acte was committed.

Thus being carefully occupyed in the bufines of the vniuerfitie, he could not yet be vnmindfull of the lady Margretes bufines: and becaufe he had no quyet refting place within the vniuerfitie to doe the fame, it was fome impediment vnto him for a longe time, for by vertue of his office of Chauncellorfhipp he had no habitacion or manfion at all belonging vnto him; Now happened it fo, that much about the fame time, Mr. Thomas Wilkinfon, doctor of Divinitie [2]and fecound Maifter of the Queene's College, departed this lyfe; which was in the yere of our lord 1505; wheruppon the fellowes of that howfe, refpecting the prefent neceffitie of this good prelate, and confideringe of his continewall dilligence and care for the whole ftate of the vniuerfitie, offered him the place of their Maifter or prefedent:

[1] Fol. 18.   [2] Fol. 18, back.

which with many thanks he accepted, and fo was third maifter of
that howfe, continewing therin the fpace of 3 yeres and odd mounthes,
and fo at times convenient he proceeded to the erection of Chriftes
College for the lady Margaret, to the endowment wherof fhe gave
lands for the maintaynance of a Maifter with xii fchollers fellowes
and xlvi difciples for ever to be brought vp (as the wordes of her
will makes mention) in learning vertue and cunninge.

Duringe the time that he was thus occupied in the lady
Margarettes bufines, and helping the vniuerfitie, it happened the
faid lady to departe this tranfitorie life at the Abbay of St. Peter in
Weftminfter to the great greefe and forow of all good men within
this realme, which was in the yere of Chrift 1519, the third of
the Calendes of Iulie, who before her departure made her Teftament
and laft will, naming for her executors, diuers great perfonages,
amonge whom this good byfhopp was chofen as one in whom her
leaft truft was not repofed.

[1] Thefe executors affembling themfelves together, to debate of
fuch things as belonged to their charge, began firft to take order for
her buriall, which they in moft folemne wife did celebrate at
Weftminfter, according to the dignitie of fuch a noble princeffe
as fhe was. And at her months minde [2] my lord of Rochefter made
a verie notable fermon in manner of a mour[n]full lamentacion,
wherin he moft gravely and lyke a worthie father fetteth forth the
noble and vertuous quallities of that bleffed woman. And for as
much as the matter therof is well worthie to be remembred, & much
the more, in that the commendacion was geven to fuch a perfon
as iuftly deferved it, by fuch a prelate as vfed not to fay haftily
more then he could well verefie, I cannot omitt to declare vnto you
the effect therof in few wordes.

In this Sermon he compareth her in four pointes to the bleffed
and noble woman Martha the fifter of marie, That is to fay, in
nobillitie of perfon, in difcipline of her body, in ordering her foul to
god, and laftly in hofpitallitie and charitable dealinge to her neigh-
bours. Firft towchinge her nobillitie, he fheweth how nobly fhe was
borne, beinge the daughter of John Duke of Somerfett, linally

[1] Fol. 19. [2] "minde" underlined & "end" written in margin.

defcended from the noble prince king Edward *the* third; and after many princly quallities, there by him declared to be in her, he concludeth, that what by linage and what by affinitie fhe had 30 kings and Queenes within the fourth degree of maryage to her, befides [1]Dukes, marqueffes, Earles, and other princes. Then for chriftian difcipline, he fetteth out how carefully fhe alwaies efchewed bankettes, rere fuppers, and Iunkettes betweene meales. And for fafting, although for her age and feeblenes fhe was not fo ftraitly bounde as others were, yet fuch daies as were by the church comaunded, fhe would dilligently keep, vfing in Lent one meale in the daie only, and that vpon a difh of fifh, befides divers other peculier faftes, which devoutly fhe obferved. And yet when fhe was in health, fhe never fayled on certaine daies in the weeke to weare fomtimes a fhirt and fomtimes a girdle of heare *that* full often her fkinn was perced therwith. Thirdly for ordering her felf to god by often kneelinge, by forrowfull weepinge, by continewall prayers and meditac*i*ons, it is almoft incredible to thinke what time fhe beftowed in them all. Info muchas fhe accuftomed her felf to ryfe co*m*monly at 5 of the clock in the morninge, bycaufe fhe would omitt no parte therof. Fourthly he magnifyeth her, for her godly & charitable hofpitallitie towards all fortes of people, & namely towards poore futors, not only in geving them meate and drinke, but alfo in helping them to an ende of their caufes, for the which fhe fuffered many a [2]rebuke. Then for poore people, wherof xii fhe daily and nightly maintayned in her howfe with meat drinke and cleathinge befides vifiting them in their ficknes, and miniftringe to them, with her owne handes, in grubbing & fearching their wounds and fores with her owne fingers, declaring evidently what her good will was to have don*n*e our faviour Jefus, yf himfelf had bene p*r*efent, feeing fhe did thus much to his fervautes for his fake: which eftfons by her owne wordes fhe verie well confirmed, when fhe would faie that yf c*hri*ftien princes would have warred vpo*n* the enemies of our faith fhe would be glad to follow the hoft and helpe to wafh their clothes for the Love of Jefus, and this fhe ftill vttered till the howre of her death. Many other great vertues and manifeft proofes

---

[1] Fol. 19, back. [2] Fol. 20.

of the fanctitie of that noble ladie he openeth in that fermon verie rare to be heard of in fuch a perfonage. But becaufe her notable actes may well require a whole volume of it felf, I will fpare to fay any further therof in this place.

When the funeralls of the lady Margaret were ended and donne, the Executors began further to confulte for execution of her will. Specially towchinge the Statutes of *Chriftes* College, and erection of St. Johns College in Cambrige, wherin becaufe my lord of Rochefter had alwais before more largly dealt then any other, they thought no man fo fitt to accomplifh that bufines as he, [1] who being the only meane and firft mover of her to fuch godly enterprifes, was alfo beft acquainted with her meaning therin: whervpon the other executors by generall confent and affent, refigned vnto him the whole authoritie, by publicke inftrument in writinge: which he for the great defire he had to fatiffie that vertuous ladies laft will in fo meritorious a caufe did not vnwillingly accept. And therfore returning to Cambrige he proceeded in that godly purpofe with great dilligence. And becaufe *Chr*iftes College was cleane furnifhed in her life time (as before is declared) the cheefe care that remayned was for the College of St. John *the* Evangelift, which was in manner nowe to be builte wholely after her death, cheefly at her coftes and charges, as by her teftament fhe had willed, although he added therto no fmall fome out of his owne purfe, for although fhe of her meere liberalitie gave by her laft will and Teftament to this College a portion of land for maintaynance of a maifter and fyftie fchollers in vertue cunning and fervice of god (as her will mentioneth), with all kind of furniture & fervantes needfull in euery office, after *the* manner and forme of other Colleges in Cambrige, yet did he not only beare a portion of the buildinge vpon his owne charge, but alfo much augmented it in poffeffions, foundinge there four fellowfhipps, a reader of an hebrew [2] lecture, a reader of a greeke lecture, four examiner readers, and four vnder readers to helpe the principall reader; and becaufe the price of victuales and other things began faft to ryfe he gave to euery one a fome of money to be weekly devided in augmenting the fellowes commons. Thus did this godly man not only beftowe his labour,

[1] Fol. 20, back. [2] Fol. 21.

care, and ftudie in executinge the will of the noble ladie the foundreffe; but alfo adde much thervnto of his owne purfe, to the accomplifhment and making perfect of that fair College, befides the wholefome ftatutes and ordinaunces moft prudently by him penned, and many godly deeds by him executed. For the continewall obferyacion and maintaynance wherof he gave good landes to the College for euer, as moft cleerly maie appeare by the auncient record which he left in wrytinge, and the ftatutes of the fame college, if fince that time they be not altered, and corrupted. Lykewife his librarie of bookes (which was thought to be fuch as no Byfhop in Europe had the lyke) with all his hangings, plate, and veffell, for hall, chamber, butterie, and kitchin, he gave longe before his death, to the College of St. John by a deed of guifte, and put the howfe in poffeffion therof by guifte of his owne handes, and then by Indenture borrowed all the faid bookes and ftuffe of them againe, to have the vfe therof during his lyfe. But at his apprehenfion all thefe things were converted an other way and fpoiled by certaine Commiffioners fent from the kinge for the fame purpofe. And for a perpetuall memorie of his [1]hartye good will and love borne towards the College, he caufed a little Chappell to be builded neere to the high Altar of the great Chappell, and fett therin a Tombe of white marble finely wrought, minding there to have refted his bodye amonge them, yf god had not afterwardes difpofed him otherwife, and for as much as of the two regions the North and the South, into which England is divided he noted the North to be more barraine of learninge, and fo ruder in manners then the Sowth, he provided in the fame Statutes that the greater part afwell of the fellowes, as of the fchollers fhould alwais be received out of the North partes: not of parcialitie and affeccion that he being borne in the north might feeme to beare to his native countrey, but in refpect of the need which he of his great wifdome and providence did eafily fee to require, wherby it is come to paffe, that thefe two Colleges (by which Cambrige is fince that time much bewtified) have not only in a fhort fpace brought forth a great number of learned men, well inftructed in all fciences and knowledge of the three learned tongues, to the finguler benefit of the Church of

[1] Fol. 21, back.

god, and commonwelth of this realme, but have alſo ſent out of them ſome holy martyrs, for in our time we may remember that famous learned fatner Mr. Richard Raynoldes, doctor of divinitie and monke profeſſed in Sion, of the rule of St. Brigett, and Mr. William Exmewe, a Carthuſian profeſſed [1] in London, both which came out of Chriſtes College and ſuffred martyrdome in the time of kinge Henrie the VIIIth; from that place ſprunge alſo that moſt reuerrend and grave doctor Maiſter Nicholas Heath Archbiſhop of Yorke, and after Chancellour of England, and Maiſter Cuthbert Scott Biſhop of Cheſter. Lykewiſe out of the College of Saint John came that famous martyr Doctor Greenwood, who ſuffered death vnder kinge Henric for the ſupremmacie: and of Biſhopps came Maiſter George [2] Daye biſhop of Chicheſter, Maiſter Raph Bayn byſhop of Litchfelde, Maiſter Thomas Watſon biſhop of Lincolne, Maiſter John Chriſtoferſon an other biſhop of Chicheſter, and Maiſter Thomas Bourcher, biſhop elect of Gloceſter, and before that Abbott of Leiſter, All right grave Devines, learned preachers and worthie Catholyke biſhops. Beſides that of Deanes in Cathedrall churches, and other learned doctors and preachers, they have brought forth ſuch an infinite number, that it is wonnder to thinke and worthie without all doubt, to be attributed principally to the goodnes and exceeding mercie of god over this realme, who againſt this wicked time of Hereſie, did even then moſt gratiouſly prepare this good ladies minde, to ſuch a notable worke of mercie, by the meanes of this ſo worthie a biſhops dilligence and faithfull carefulnes to execute the ſame, which providence of god appeareth plainly in that within ſo ſhort a time as paſſed betweene the erection of the Colleges and the rayſing of the ſciſme, it was poſſible for ſo many worthie and Catholick learned men to ſpring out of ſo ſmall a fountaine. And as by the great liberallitie and bountie of this noble & [3] bleſſed woman the vniuerſitie of Cambrige doth now at this preſent remaine much advaunced in the faculties of ſtudie and learninge, ſo may we note, how that of longe time, even as it were from her firſt begininge, it hath pleaſed god to move the hartes of ſundrie noble

---

[1] Fol. 22.
[2] Richard originally written, then scratched out and George written over.
[3] Fol. 22, back.

Catholick kings and queenes of the Realme, with other noble princes of the blood royall, to put to their benevolent and helping handes. Infomuch that through their gratious and bountifull charitie, proceedinge no doubt of efpeciall favour and affeccion, which they in their feuerall ages have ever borne to this vniuerfitie, it is at this daie adorned with many goodly colleges, bewtifyed with diuers fumptuous churches and Chappells, and plentifully endowed with landes and poffeffions wherby she hath norifhed and brought forth many fingulerly well learned in all faculties of knowlege and learninge, wherin as fhe hath alwais wonne praife and commendacions, fo hath fhe moft of all deferved in this one pointe : That in fo many hundred yeres as fhe hath florifhed, never herefie, nor other vnfound doctrine hath fpronge out of any of her members, wherby the Catholick Church of Chrift hath at any time bene difturbed, But alwais hath perfevered in found doctrine, yea, even then moft of all when Oxford her Sifter, the other vniuerfitie, was miferably toffed and turmoyled with the peftiferous herefies and fectes of wicklef. For we maie reade of diuers learned clerkes fometimes fchollers and ftudientes of this vniuerfitie [1] of Cambrige that have in their feverall times learnedly confuted, and moft carefully rooted out, fuch pernitious herefies as then were difperfed as well in this realme as els where. And even now in thefe our daies there have not wanted fundrie learned fathers of that number, befides this moft reuerend and holy doctor of whom we now intreat, that have ftept forth againft thefe damnable errors and fectes now troobling this realme, and the whole world befides, by whofe learning and dilligence it is not vnlyke, but this realme might have bene fafely preferved, had not the kinge himfelf bene firft infected with this fowle and horrible fpott of herefie, who by his owne vnlawfull power, not only removed from their places all thefe auncient and fage rules [2] that fhould by their learning and grave authoritie have repulfed fuch pernitious fectes, but alfo placed in their roomes fuch and fo manie heretickes as himfelf had chofen, to fet forward his wicked and execrable purpofes. And as it is not to be reade of any hereticke by them brought forth of their owne flocke and number; So have

[1] Fol. 23.   [2] rulers. Harleian, 250, 6896, 7049.

they not willingly fuffred any other Heretick of forrain nation or countrey to abide quyetly amonge them; wherof although diuers examples might be recyted, yet can I not omitt this one being yet frefh in memorie. To witt, of M. B. and P. F.,[1] two wicked and pernitious heretickes, who although in the childifh raigne of king Edward the VIth when they and all others of their profeffion, did frankly profeffe and openly teach within that vniuerfitie whatfoeuer pleafed themfelves even to their dying daies, and being borne out by the power of [2]fuch as then ruled all at their licentious wills and pleafures, wherby a great part of the youth of that time refident there at ftudie were much anoyed and infected with their peftilent herefies. Yet lacked there not many even at that inftant of the elder fort, which not fo ftoutly as learnedly, yea in open difputacion impugned their devilifh doctrine, and would not have failed to hiffe them out of their fchooles, had they not by fwaie of that time bene put to filence, fome by banifhment, and other fome by imprifonment. And yet in the time of good Queene Marie, when thefe and fuch lyke learned and reuerend men were reftored againe, to their accuftomed eftate of governement within that vniuerfitie. They, mindfull of their dutye and carefull to fupply the want which the iniquitie of the time would not before permitt them to attempt according to the holy Cannons of the Church, caufed not only the carcaffes and bones of thofe heretickes to be vnburied, and taken out of the grave, wherof at their death they were not capable by lawe, but alfo, for example fake, by lawfull authoritie procured the fame bones and carcaffe then to be openly burnt in the marked place in the face of the worlde, that for the enormitie of their haynous crime, the dead bodies and bones might beare witnes of their punifhment, which they yet livinge by lawe deferved, and fhould have felt by all lykelyhood, yf (as I have faid) the iniquitie of the time had not letted. He alfo minded to have erected [3]yet a third College in Cambrige of his proper charges, and therin confulted with Erafmus by fundrie epiftles for his advife: but becaufe he was prevented by the iniquitie of time that fhortly after followed, in which his goods began to waft, he left of his purpofe and neuer began it at all.

[1] Martin Bucer, Paulus Fagius *in margin*.   [2] Fol. 23, back.   [3] Fol. 24.

Now approched the time wherin God was determined to make triall of his people, the man of finne (Antichrift) fhould be yet more manifeftly revealed, for the verie mouth of hell was fett open, and out came the wicked fpirit of Antichrift and entred into Martin Luther, an Auguftin frier, an infamous heretick and execrable Apoftata. This wicked man fet forth diuers blafphemous bookes ftuffed with moft abhominable and falfe doctrines, which in fhort time came to the fight of my lord of Rochefter ; whervpon he began not only to fette himfelf to more dilligent preaching and wryting then euer he had yet done before, but alfo procured and fet forward many other learned preachers to looke and forefee that this cruell and ravenous wolfe fhould not devour England, and by occafion therof provided in the ftatutes of Saint John's college before mentioned, that the fellowes of the howfe fhould fo order and moderate their ftudies, as alwais the fourth part of them might be prechers, and as foone as one was gone abroad an other fhould ftraight waies be readie to fucceed in his place. Thus he ftill occupied himfelf ether privatly or openly, never intermitting the fpirituall care of his dioceffe, whether he were at London or at Cambrige, [1] or els where, fpecially now when the wicked feed of Luther was fo faft fowen and difperfed abroade. For this caufe he returned to his charge at Rochefter, being then at Cambrige, and after he had there remayned a certaine fpace, preaching and teaching after his accuftomed fafhion, he was taken with great defire to travell to Rome, there to falute the Pope's holines, and to vifitt the toumbes of the holy Apoftles Saint Peter and Saint Paul, with the reft of the holy places and reliques there. But you fhall vnderftand that this was not the firft time that he had entred into that deliberacion ; for it was by him determined from the time that he firft received his Bifhoprick, which by certaine occafions was twife before difapointed. Wherfore havinge now gotten (as he thought) a good opportunitie, he providently difpofed his howfehould and all his other matters : and after leave obtained of the kinge and his metropolitan, he began to prepare for his iorney to Rome : to this voyage he had chofen learned companio. But beholde, when euerie thing was readie and

[1] Fol. 24, back.

the iorney about to begin, all was fodenly difapointed, and he
revoked, for other bufines to be treated of at home, which of neceffitie
required his prefence. And this (without all doubt) was not without
the providence of Almightie God, who, content with his good minde,
thought not that iorney then expedient. Being then thus ftaid &
lette l to proceed in his devout purpofe, he returned where he [1]lefte
to his paftorall cure at Rochefter, wherof at that time was great
neede, for the wicked fect of Luther grewe verie fafte ; the caufe of
his revocacion was by meane of a Synod of byfhopps called by
Cardinall Woolfey who (having lately before received his power
legantine from the Pope) at that time ruled all things vnder the kinge
alfo at his owne will and pleafure. To this Sinod the Clergie of
England affembled themfelves in great number, where it was expected
that great matters for the benefitt of the Church of England fhould
have been propaned, howbeit all fell out otherwife: for (as it
appeared after) This Counfell was called by my Lord Cardinall rather
to notifie to the world his great authoritie, and to be feene fitting in
his Pontificiall feate, then for any great good that he ment to doe
which this learned and wife prelate perceived quickly. Wherfore
having now good occafion to fpeake againft fuch enormities as he faw
daily ryfinge amonge the fpiritualtie and much the rather for that his
wordes were amonge the Clergie aloane, without any commixture of
the layitie, which at that time began to hearken to any fpeaking
againft the Clergie, he there reprooved verie difcreetly the ambition
and incontinencie of the Clergie, utterly condemninge their vanitie,
in wearing of Coftly apparrell, wherby he declared the goods of the
Church to be finfully wafted & fcandall to be rayfed amonge the
people, feeing the tythes and other oblacions geven by the devotion
of them, and their anceftors, to a good purpofe fo inordinately fpent
in [2]vndecent and fuperfluous rayment, delicate fare, and other worldly
vanitie, which matter he debated fo largly and framed his wordes
after fuch fort, that the Cardinall perceiued himfelf to be towched to
the verie quicke : for he affirmed this kind of diforder to proceed
through the example of the head, and thervpon reprooved his Pomp,
putting him in minde, that it ftood better with the modeftie of fuch

[1] Fol. 25.   [2] Fol. 25, back.

a high paftor as he was to efchewe all worldly vanitie; fpecially in this perilous time. And by humillitie to make himfelf conformable and lyke the Image of god, "for in this trade of lyfe" (faid he) "how can there be any lykelyhood of perpetuitie with fafetie of confcience, nether yet any fecuritie of the Clergie to continewe, but fuch plaine and imminent daungers are lyke to enfewe, as were neuer tafted nor heard of before our daies: for what fhould we" (faid he) "exhort our flockes to efchew and fhunn worldly ambition, when we our felves that be byfhopps, do wholely fett our mindes to the fame things we forbidd in them. What example of Chrift our faviour do we imitate, who firft executed doing and after fell to teachinge. Yf we teach accordinge to our doinge, how abfurd may our doctrine be accounted; yf we teache one thinge and doe another, our labour in teaching fhall never benefitt our flocke half fo much as our example in doing fhall hurt them. Who can willingly fuffer and beare with vs in whom (preaching humilitie, fobrietie, and contempt of the world) they maie evidently perceive, hawtines in minde, pride in gefture, fumptuoufnes in apparell, and damnable exceffe in all worldly delicates. Truly, moft reuerend fathers, what this vanitie in temporall things worketh in you I know not, but fure I am that in my felfe I perceive a greate impediment to devotion, and fo have felt a longe time, for fundrie times when I have fetled and fully bent my felf to the care of my flocke committed vnto me, to vifitt my dioceffe, to governe my church, and to anfwere the enemies of Chrift, ftraight ways hath come a meffenger for one caufe or other fent from higher authoritie, by whom I have bene called to other bufines and fo left of my former purpofe. And thus by toffing and going this waie and that way time hath paffed, and in the meane while nothinge done, but attending after tryvmphs, receiving of Ambaffadors, haunting of princes courtes, and fuch lyke, wherby great expenfes ryfe that might better be fpent otherwaie." He added further, that whereas himfelf, for fundrie caufes fecretly knowne to himfelf, was thrife determined to make his voyage to Rome, and at everie time had taken full and perfect order for his cure, his howfhould, and for all other bufines, till his returne, ftill by occafion of thefe worldly

[1] Fol. 26.

matters, he was difapointed of his purpofe. After he had vttered thefe with many moe fuch words in this Sinod, they feemed all by their filence to be much aftonyed, and to thinke well of his fpeeches, but in deede, [1] by the fequell of the matter, it fell out that fewe were perfwaded by his counfell, for noe man vpon this amended any whitt of his accuftomed licentious lyfe, no man became one heare the more circumfpect or watchfull over his cure, and many were of this mind, that they thought it nothing neceffarie for them to abate anythinge of their faire apparell for the reprehenfion of a fewe whom they thought too fcrvpelous : fo that (excufes neuer wantinge to cover finn :) this holy fathers wordes, fpoken with fo good a zeale, were all loft, and came to nothinge for that time.

In the meane fpace Luthers herefie ftill proceeded, fpreading farr and wide abroad in Saxsonie, and other dominions of Germanie, and the poyfoned bookes therof at laft came frefhly into England, by the helpe of marchantes that travelled that waie : by meane wherof not they themfelves only, but alfo artificers, foldiers, women, and other of the common people, fpecially of the yonger fort, fimply learned, and of little vnderftanding, by readinge thefe bookes, ftraight waies at the firft receipt dranke their deadly draught of this venomous poyfon. Then after it crept abroad lyke a canker more largly, and entred into the minde of many englifh people of the better fort, who, lyke the nature of Iflanders that commonly be changeable and defirous of novelties, received yt with much plawfibillitie, which [2] thinge king Henrie confideringe, he ftraight waie without delay called for helpe to the Bifhopps, and imediatly with his owne penn fett vpon Luther, the head of all the mifcheef, by meane wherof, he not only fhewed himfelf well to deferve the name of defendor of the faith (which after vpon occafion of that booke was geven him by our holy father Pope Leo the tenth) but alfo brought amonge the learned byfhops of his owne realme, a great hope, that by his helpe all would be ftaied for that time. That booke of the kings (which was a right worthie and learned treatife) was intituled an affertion of the feaven facraments againft Martyn Luther.

There were at that time diuers that would affirme my lord of

[1] Fol. 26, back.   [2] Fol. 27.

Rochefter to be author of that booke, for certaine it is, that in thofe daies no man was greater with the king in *that* kind of bufines then he: nether did *the* king yelde more reuerence or credit to any man living then to him. In fo much as he would many times faie, that he thought him the deepeft divine in Europe, which doth nothinge at all detract from the kings praife, but rather maketh the booke more commendable, even as thofe wife and fubftantiall lawes which the king doth make by advife of his learned counfellors do nothing derogate from his authoritie, but are promulged and publifhed for his owne ordinaunces. He further, to the advauncment of the kings worthines and defence of the truth againft that bitter poyfond anfwere of Luther, made an appollogie, rebuking Luther as well for his fcurrillitie and knavifh tearmes vfed againft fo noble a prince as alfo for his falfe and manifeft errors, which he moft profoundly confuteth. The publifhing of which booke [1] he deferred for a time, becaufe the rumor was that Luther would recante. But when it was perceived that he with all his factors, with all their might ceafed not to vrge forward the fcifme, fetting forth corrupted tranflacion of bibles, and wreftinge the fence therof to their owne malitious vnderftandinge, he fetteth his booke immediatly forth, for a warninge to all pofteritie, with a preface before yt, to his ould acquaintance the Bifhop of Elie, named Doctor Weft, being both brought vp together from their youth in ftudie at Cambrige, where many difputacion had paffed betweene them, as partly in the faid preface himfelf doth remember, the infcription of which booke was thus: A defence of the kinge of Englands affertion of the Cath. faith againft Martin Luthers booke of the Captiuitie of Babulon. About the fame time he was alfo compilinge an other booke, wherin he defended the holy order of preifthood againft Luther, and fett yt to the printe. Thus lamenting with himfelf the prefent ftate of things, and devifing how to provide remedie for that which he fawe followinge, lyke to a carefull Shepherde he laid watch in everie corner, fearching all places where the enemye might enter, and where any came within his reach, he tooke houlde on them, fpecially againft the Lutherans, he exalted his voice lyke a trumpett preaching againft them more

[1] Fol. 27, back.

liberallie, and alfo more often then his former cuftome was. Befides, forth he fent [1] abroade certaine other preachers, men well inftructed to catch the woolfe and to admonifh the people of the fecrett poyfon that laye hidd, under pretext of reformacion. But behould, how eafie a thinge it is to deceive the fillie people, and how quickly they that be light of Credit, maie be induced to followe crooked waies and bye pathes: for they geving care to flaunderous tales and pernitious lyes develifhly invented by Luther vpon abufes attributed to the Clergie, and cleane carryed awaie with carnall libertie, which this new fifth gofpell did liberallie bringe them, were fallen in that wilfull blindnes, that making themfelves iudges in that which they fhould receive by iudgment of their paftors, nether by the kings affertion againft Luther, nether by the continewall vifitac[i]ons of their byfhopps, neither yet by the dilligent and faithfull teaching of the learned fathers and doctors, could be ftaide, but altogether drunken with the Mufte of licentious libertie fo frankly broached vnto them, and wilfully wedded to their vaine prefumption, rafhly and without reafon, they fuffred themfelves to be abufed by that falfe and wicked heretick (whom they fhould moft dilligently have efchewed), and imbraced him as a trewe and fyncere reformer of vice, calling him a holy father, a trew and godly preacher of gods worde, yea, a verie prophett. This did they firft by whifperinge fecretly amonge themfelves, then by open talke, and at length by open cafting abroade and vfing his feditious booke pernitioufly penned to catch the ignorant fort, by abafing the authoritie of the Pope, Kings, and Bifhops, and all other potentates. Of this faction were fix at one time apprehended, wherof the [2] cheefe was Robert Barnes, an Auguftine freer, which after longe perfwafion of diuers learned men abiured their falfe and deteftable herefies, and for their pennaunce ftood openly at Paules Croffe on the quinquagefima Sundaie, which was in the yere of our redemption 1525. At which time this learned byfhop made there a worthie fermon, where the moft reuerend father Maifter Thomas Wolfey, Cardinall and legate a latere with xi bifhopps, and a great audience of people were prefent. In which fermon he there profecuted the gofpell, vttering it againft the lutherans fectes

---

[1] Fol. 28.   [2] Fol. 28, back.

with fuch fervencie of faith, fuch zeal to the Catholick Church of *Chrift*, fuch force of argumentes grounded vppon holy fcripture, and fo fully replenifhed with the holy ghoft, that yf the king had bene as trewe a Defender of the faith in his deedes, as he was in name and tytle, no doubt but England had bene fafe & foundly preferved from that miferable crime that after yt fell into. He pronounced an other notable Sermon verie fhortly after before the faid lord Cardinall in the fame place, within the Octaves of the Affention, in which he fhewed himfelf a ftowt and zealous preacher, and a moft vigilant paftor againft thefe raveninge and peftiferous heretickes; many other Sermons and homilies to the fame effect he made, befides, at London the head cittie of England, taking therby occafion to taxe afwell the negligence of Curates, as the rafhnes and levitie of the people, exhorting all forts in their vocacion to play the vigilant foldiers in ftowtly refiftinge thefe develifh affaultes of herefie.

[1]Now after this his wearifome occupacion of preachinge there followed yet an other painfull labour of wrytinge, for at this time rofe out of Luthers fchoole Oecolampadius, who lyke a mightie Giant braft out more venomoufly, (if more could be) then his *Maifter*, Freer Luther. For thinking himfelf better learned then his Maifter, he went an afe further, denying damnably the reall prefence of the bodie and blood of our faviour in the bleffed facrament of the Altar, wherin as he went altogether from his mother the Church, so did he differ farr from his fchoolemaifter, Martin Luther, wherfore the grave prelate & zelous paftor, lyke a valiant Champion (that never could be tyred), fet vpon this raveninge woolf with five weapons, which were fiue bookes moft dilligently and clerkly collected, well ftuffed with evident fcriptures, and cenfures of holy fathers, both in their learned works, and alfo in their generall Counfells where lawfully affembled, they have declared fuch things as are expedient for the maintaynance of the truth reprefenting our mother the Church, by the authoritie and vertue wherof he fo wounded this Golias, that in conclufion he cleane ouerthrewe him and laid him flatt on the ground. Thefe bookes were written in the yere of *Chrift* 1525, at which time he had governed the Sea of

[1] Fol. 29.

Rochefter about twenty yeres, and the next yere followinge they were publifhed and fett abroad in print, to the great confirmacion of all good [1] *Chriftians*, that ether read or heard the fame, and no leffe difcorrage of all heretickes, as by the fequell maie well appeare, for nether to thofe bookes, nether yet to any other of his bookes or workes hath any heretick to this daie yet made anfwere or refutacion, which I thinke can hardly be faid of any other Catholyke wryter that wrote in his time.

Hitherto we have difcribed vnto you this worthie prelate, nether doombe in preachinge, nor ydle in wryting : nether could in devotion, nor ambitious in afpyringe. It followeth now that we muft intreate of a great and lamentable calamitie that chaunced in thefe our daies, wherof as I thinke there are verie few that can fay they have cleane efcaped without feelinge fome part of the fmart, fo this reuerend father tafted plentifully therof, whom yt chaunced in the verie begining to be one of the firft that brake the yfe, and to open and fhewe the inconvenience that followed therby, no doubte to his immortall fame and glorie, and no leffe to the reproach and ignominie of all fuch as were his perfecutors, as by the fequell of this Hyftory fhall well appeare. I meane here of the Divorce between kinge Henrye and queen Katherine his wife : the verie Spring from which fo many lamentable & miferable tragedies have fpronge, to the vtter ruine and defolacion of [2] this noble Realme of England, in the trew fervice of god, and miniftracion of Juftice, and knowledge of all ciuill honeftie. So that befides the greefe, and loathfomnes therof I thinke it a matter almoft vnpoffible to be expreffed in wrytinge, But forafmuch as the worthie Actes of this holy father cannot plainly be vnderftoode, vnleffe we enter fomwhat into this matter nether this matter fully perceived except we make a little digreffion, yet it fhall be convenient, to repeat from the firft origenall and fountaine, the caufe of all this greevous bufines, wherin yf I fhall feeme fomwhat prolixe and tedeous, I muft defire the reader to confider the fruite which he maie reape by the full difcourfee therof, being full of profitable and vertuous leffons and good examples.

There hath of longe time continewe l an auncient amitie and

[1] Fol. 29, back. [2] Fol. 30.

frendſhipp, between the howſe of Burgundie and this Realme of England, wherby amonge other commodities, great traffique of marchandize from the one countrey to the other hath vſually bene practiſed: to the which howſe of Burgundie when in proceſſe of time, the noble families of Auſtria, Spaine, Naples, and Sicilie was by maryage adioyned, the moſt ſage and vertuous prince Kinge Henrie the vii[th], perceiving ſo many noble kingdoms and countreys now brought to one Monarchie, and therwith much deſiringe the continewance of his auncient league and amitie aforetime vſed, ſent vnto Ferdinando, King of Aragon and Caſtile, requiring of him in marryage, the lady Catherine his daughter for the lord Arthur, prince of wales, his eldeſt ſonne.

[1] Kinge Ferdinando (as he was a wife and noble prince) ſo in this matter he ſhewed himſelf nether hard nor ſtrange, but ſtraight waies agreed to this good motion. Then was preparacion made for the iorney, and the noble yonge ladie beinge imbarked and arived in England, was at laſt ſolemnly marryed to the ſaid Prince Arthur in the Cathedrall church of Saint Paul within London: which was in the yere of our lord god 1500, and the xvi[th] yere of King Henrie the ſeventh his Raigne. After the ſolemnitie of the marryage was finiſhed they went both to Ludlowe, in Shropſhire, and there for a ſpace remayned, and kept howſe together. But beholde (god ſo orderinge the matter) within five monnths after the marryage, Prince Arthur beinge alwais but a weake and ſickly yonge man not above the age of xv yeres chaunced to depart this tranſitorie life, by meane wherof, the good intent and meaning of the two kings their fathers, was nowe become all fruſtrat and void. Neuertheles that ſo good a matter, ſo well begun, ſhould not altogether quaile, there was yet an other waie deviſed how all might be ſolved againe, and the firſt good intention take place: This was, that feeing the ladie Catherine was now a widdowe without yſſue of Prince Arthur her huſband, ſhe might therefore be married to the lorde Henrie, brother to the ſaid prince. Of this deviſe both the kings lyked well, and to that inclyned their mindes accordingly, & leſt ſome cavillacion might in time ariſe about this matter, bycauſe of the Leviticall lawe, ſor-

---

[1] Fol. 30, back.

bidding the one brother [1] to reveale the fecrettes of the other, yt was thought good by the learned counfell on both fides that difpenfacion fhould be fewed for from the Sea apoftolick, which was done and graunted accordinge to the two kings requeftes by our holy father Pope Julius the fecond. In this Bull the maryage with Prince Henrie was difpenced, for that the ladie was before maryed to his brother prince Arthur, yea, in cafe there were carnall knowledge between them.

The tenore wherof was thus.

Julius epifcopus feruus feruorum dei.

Dilecto filio Henrico chariffimo in Chrifto filii nostri Henrici Angliæ regis illuftris Nato: et dilecte Catherinæ chariffimi in Christo filij nostri Ferdinandi regis, et chariffimæ filiæ Elizabethæ reginæ Hifpaniarum et Siciliæ catholicorum natæ illuftribus Salutem, &c.

Romani pontificis præcellens authoritas confeffa fibi defuper utimur poteftate provt perfonarum negotiorum & temporum qualitate penfata in domino confpicit falubriter expedire.

Oblata nobis nuper pro parte vestra petitionis feries continebat, quod cum alias tam in Christo filia Catherina & tunc in humanis agens quondam Arthurus chariffimi in Christo filij nostri—Henrici Anliæ regis illuftris: primogenitus pro conferuandis pacis et amicitæ nexibus et federibus, inter chariffimum in Christo filium nostrum Ferdinandum et chariffimam in Christo filiam nostram Elizabetham Hifpaniarum et Siciliæ reginam Catholicos; ac præfatos Angliæ [2] reges et reginam matrimonium legitime per verba de prefenti contraxiffetis, illudque carnali copula forfan confummaviffetis dictus Arthurus prole ex hujufmodi matrimonis non fufcepta defeffit. Cum autem ficut eadem petitio fubiungebat ad hoc, vt vinculum pacis et amiciciæ inter præfatos regem et reginam hujufmodi diutius permaneat, cupiatis matrimonium inter vos per verba legitime de prefenti contrahere: Supplicari nobis feciftis, vt vobis in premiffis de oportunæ difpenfacionis gratia providere; de benignitate apoftolica dignaremur.

Nos igitur qui inter fingulos Christi fideles ac prefertim catholicos reges et principes, pacis et concordiæ amœnitatem vrgere intenfis

[1] Fol. 31.   [2] Fol. 31, back.

deſiderijs affectamus : Vos et quemlibet ve*s*trum, a quibufcunq*ue* excomm*uni*cati*o*n*i*bus &c. : Hu*juſmo*di fupplicac*i*onibus inclinati, vos bifcunq*ue* vt (impedimento affinitatis hu*juſmo*di ex premiſſis proveniente ac conſtitutionib*us* et ordinac*i*on*i*bus a*pos*t*o*licis cæterifq*ue* co*n*trarijs nequaquam obſtantibus) matrimoniu*m* per verba le*gi*time de præſen*ti* inter vos contrah*e*re, et in eo poſtquam contractum fuerit et ſi iam forſan hactenus de facto publice vel clandeſtine contraxeritis ac illud carnali copula confumm*a*ueritis, licite remanere valeatis authoritate a*pos*t*o*lica, tenore presentiu*m* de fpir*i*tualis dono graciæ difpenfamus, ac vos et quemlibet ve*s*trum ſi contraxeritis, vt praefertur[1] ab exceſſu hu*juſmo*di excomm*uni*cac*i*on*i*s fententia quam propterea incurristis eadem authoritate [2] abfoluimus prolem ex hu*juſmo*di matrimonio ſiue contracto ſiue contrahendo fufceptam forfan vel fufcipiendam le*gi*timam decerendo.

Proviso quod tu in C*hri*sto filia Catherina propter hu*juſmo*di rapta non fueris, volumus autem ſi hu*juſmo*di matrimoniu*m* de facto co*n*traxeritis Confeſſor per vos et quemlibet ve*ſt*rum eligendus penitentiam falutarem propterea vobis iuiungat, quam adimplere teneamini. Nulli ergo &c. Datu*m* Romæ etc., 1507, calend*is* Januarij, Anno &c., which in english may be thus underſtoode :

Julius Byſhopp, Servant to *th*e fervantes of god. To our loving fonne Henrie, the fonne of our moſt deere fonne in C*h*riſt, Henri the noble king of England. And to our beloved daughter in Chriſt, Catherine the daughter of our moſt deere fonne and daughter Ferdinando and Elizabeth, the Catholyke king and queene of Spain and Sicilie, greeting, &c. The Biſhop of Rome by his high authorytie geven vnto him from above doth vſe his power, waying the quallitie of the perſons, the buſines, & the time, as he feeth expedient and profitable in our lorde. There hath lately ben preſented vnto vs a petition on yo*u*r behalf contayninge that where you our welbeloved daughter Katherin and Arthur then livinge, the eldeſt fonne of our moſt deere fonne in C*h*riſt Henrie the noble kinge [3] of England, had (for confervac*i*on of the bondes and pactes of peace and amitie between our moſt deere fonne and daughter

---

[1] præfertur, Harleian, 7049 and 250; MS. peſertur.   [2] Fol. 32.
[3] Fol. 32, back.

Ferdinando and Elizabeth, Catholicke king and queene of Spaine and Sicilie, and the forefaid king and queene of England) lawfully contracted between you a matrimony by prefent wordes, and had alfo perhaps confummate the fame by carnall knowledge, the faid Arthur deceaffed without any yffue borne of the fame matrimonie. And wheras you defire to contract a lawfull matrimonie betweene you by prefent words, to the intent that the bonde of peace and amitie fhould be the more durable betweene the faid king and queene. And made petition vnto vs alfo that we would vouchfafe to provide for you in the premiffes with convenient difpenfacion, by the grace and bounty of the Sea Apoftolick as in the faid fupplicacion and mentioned, we therefore, (who with erneft defire do affect the advauncment of bleffed peace and concord, amonge all Chriften people, fpecially between Catholyke kings and princes) tendering that your fupplicacion do abfolve you, and euery of you from all manner of excomunicacion, &c. And do by authority of the Sea Apoftolicke, according to the tenore of thefe prefentes, difpence with you and euery of you by the guift of fpirituall grace, that you may contract between you a matrimonie by prefent wordes, and after the fame fo contracted, ether openly or fecretly, and by carnall confent confummated, that ye may therin lawfully remaine, any [1] impediment of affinitie growing by the premiffes, or any conftitucion or ordinaunce apoftolyke or other contrarie provifions notwithftanding. And yf ye have fo contracted as before is declared we alfo doe by the fame authoritie abfolve you and euery of you from fuch exceffe and fentence of excomunicacion wherin you be runne by mean of the fame, decreeing the yffue of fuch matrimonie ether contracted or to be contracted, for lawfull, yea, although the fame be already borne. Provided alwaies that you our daughter in Chrifte Catherine were not rapt againft your will. And we will that yf ye have alreadie contracted any fuch matrimonie, the Confeffor by you or any of you to be chofen fhall inioyn you holefome pennance for the fame, to the performance wherof ye fhall be bound. No man therfore, &c., and yf they fhall &c., Geven at Rome &c. 1507 the Calendes of Januarie in the yere &c.

[1] Fol. 33.

The two kings having thus with their great charges obtained this Bull, thought now that all things were well provided for, and all matters of confcience throughly difpenfed, and then refted no more but the folemnifation of the marryage, before the accomplifhing wherof, it chaunced the forefaid fage pringe[1] king Henrie the vii[th] to depart this worlde, leaving behinde him to fucceede in the kingdome his only fonne Henrie the eight, who followinge the conclufion of his fathers agreement, efpowfed the faid ladie in the Cathedral Church of Saint Paul in London, within two months after he began to raigne, and begat of her Henrie & diuers other fonnes, which dyed in fhort fpace after [2]they were borne, and marie who in proceffe of time fucceeded in the Crowne. In this maryage they continewed & lived well and profperoufly together almoft the fpace of twentie yeres, all things in this Realme fo well fucceedinge, as the lyke hath neuer fince bene feene. But Sathan the comon enemie of all mankind, who ftill envyeth his profperitie and ioyeth at his woe, perceiving what great good was lyke to infewe to the Chriftian world by the continewance of this maryage, and how lykely his owne kingdome was therby to abate in the hartes of Chriften men, he fo wrought and beftirred himfelf in this matter, that contrarie to mans expectacion and the two noble princes good and vertuous intention, there followed in ftedd of tranquillitie and peace an vtter ruine and miferie. For in all this great profperitie behould even fodenly what a foare flame was kindled of one little fparke, by reafon of a fcruple crept into the kinges breft, that the maryage between him and this good queen his wife fhould not be lawfull bycaufe fhe was before maried to his brother. How this foolifh and vnhappie fcruple entred firft into his head, I will not certainly affirme, becaufe I have heard yt diuerfly reported. Some thinking it came by the Bifhopp of Bayon, who being on a time Ambaffador to this king Henrie from Frauncis the french kinge, to treat of a maryage betwene the lady Marie daughter to king Henrie, and the Duke of Orleans fecond fonne to the faid king of fraunce named Henry, [3]even as the matter after longe debatinge was come to determinacion, the Bifhop defired refpite of concluding the matrimonie, till fuch time as he had

[1] Prince, Harleian 6896. [2] Fol. 33, back. [3] Fol. 34.

once againe fpoken with the kinge his maifter, becaufe (as he faid) he was not fully perfwaded of the legitimacion of the ladie Marie beinge the kings daughter begotten of his brothers wife, which wordes the kinge fecretly marked, and neuer after forgott. Others haue fuppofed that it was a thinge but only conceved of the kinge himfelf, who perceivinge that he had noe iffue male by the Queene, and doubtinge now that he was lyke to haue none at all by her, (fhe growing towards the age of fortie yeres), began to conceive a wearines of her perfon, and fo fought meanes to be rydd of her, and to marrie a new wife, and for furthering of his purpofe thought it a good colour & cleanly excufe to aleadge the trooble of his confcience, and the daunger that might infewe to this Realme, for lacke of iffue male. But moft have affirmed, that this matter was firft put into his head, by an envious prowde man (then rulinge mightilie in this realme) called Maifter Thomas Wolfey, Cardinall and Archbifhop of Yorke: which I take to have moft Semblaunce of trewth for fundrie reafons, and the rather for that the good queen openly charged him fore therwith as after fhall be [1] declared, and therfore no doubt but he found out the truth therof. My felfe have alfo feene and reade diuers and fundrie letters, written from the Cardinall to the kings ambaffadors at Rome, when he afpired to be Pope: wherin he feemed nothing to favour this good queene, and therfore labored the more ernefttly to be Pope, becaufe he ment to give definitive fentence againft her to pleafure the kinge withall. This Cardinall as he lacked noe excellencie of witt, readines of fpeech, and quicknes of memorie: fo was he alfo nether faint of corrage, nor ignorant of civill manners, ne yet all vnlearned, for he had ftudied and taken degrees of Schoole in the vniuerfitie of Oxford. Of parentage he was bafe and obfcure, and yet neuertheles wanted noe audacitie to advaunce himfelf amonge great perfonages, yea in matters of great importance and waight, for in continewance of time, befides his great and rich promotion in the Church, which were nether fmall nor fewe, he was alfo lord Chancellor of England, and therby in temporall matters ruled all vnder the king at his owne will and pleafure, fo that what by the one and what by the other, he was accounted the richeft Cardinall in

[1] Fol. 34, back.

revennews and goods that euer ¹was in England. And in deed
although in his great authoritie he wonne at many wife mens hands
great praife for his indifferencie fhewed to all perfons as well rich as
poore without refpect of dignitie, gouerninge the Realme many yeres
vnder the king in great peace and tranquillitie : yet for the obfcuring
and darkninge of all thefe goodly guyfts of good nature, this one
falt of ambition (lackinge not the companie of fome other vices)
raigned fo abundantly in him that his goodnes was not thought able
to furmount the one halfe of his ill. But now by meanes of this
Cardinalls forwardnes in fervice, and much takinge vpon him it was
thought by iudgment of many wife men (as myfelf have heard fome
report, and cannot without greefe reherfe againe) that the king fell
then to ydlenes and reft, geuinge his minde to wanton love and
fenfuall pleafure, and fo with expences of his treafure and loffe of
his time gave ouer the kingly occupacion (wherin he had fo longe
before vertuoufly exercifed himfelf with the great commendacion of
all men) and lefte all to the miniftrie and difpofition of the Cardinall,
which he willingly tooke vpon him, fetting himfelf then daily forward
to the worlde with great pompe more then he had before vfed. And
yet befides his owne great fumpt & expenfes in wearing of filke and
other coftly apparrell decked with gould and filuer, he was alfo therby
occafion to other of the Clergie to doe the lyke beyond all reafon
and meafure, ²for by reafon of his great revennewes he lived rather
lyke a king then a fubiect, having in his handes all at one inftant
of fpirituall livings, the Archbifhopricke of Yorke, the Bifhopricke
of winchefter, and the Abbay of Saint Albones. He had alfo in
Farme the bifhopricke of Bathe, worcefter, and Hereford, becaufe the
incumbentes therof were ftraungers and continewally abfent in their
owne Countreys : by reafon wherof, he had the full difpofition of all
the fpirituall promotions and prefentacions in thofe Bifhoppricks, as
freely as any of his owne, befides this he was Legate de latere, by
vertue wherof he would convocate the clergie of this Realme at his
pleafure, and vifitt all fpirituall howfes & miniftrie of the Church,
and for that purpofe had officers and magiftrates throughout the
realme, and would prefent to all benefices whom he pleafed, to his

¹ Fol. 35.   ² Fol. 35, back.

owne no fmall gaine and profitt. It is alfo thought that he had out of Fraunce a yerely pention, and whether he received any thinge out of Italie for his dignitie of Cardinall or no, it is vncertaine. It were a longe matter to reherfe all the feculer bufines wherin he wrapped himfelf and the Luker which he received [1] by the fame. But the moft lamentable thinge to be remembred is this, that being in all this authoritie, he fhewed himfelf in his counfell verie inconftant, and made fmall account of the confervacion of the trewe Amitie & frendfhip between princes, for therin he preferred his owne ambitious will before the common peace and tranquillitie of Chriften nations. By which manner of doings he procured many great and lamentable tragedies in Chriftendome, and vnto himfelf the hatred of many good people, and fpecially of the good and vertuous ladie queene Katherin, wife to king Henrie the eight, and lykewife of the noble Emperour Charles the fifte, her nephewe by the fifters fide. And yet (god be thanked) I have bene crediblie informed by fundrie good and wife perfonages that were about him and knewe much of his fecrettes, that after he once efpyed the fequell of his doinges he lived in great forrowe and repentance for the fame all his lyfe after. And being at Yorke a yere or more before his death in the kings heavie difpleafure, he there lamented all the while that ever he flattered fo much with the kinge, and neglected the difpleafure of Almightie god. And to that effect he alfo fent a meffage to the kinge a litle before his death by Sir William Kingfton, then Conftable of the towre, defyring him for gods fake to proceed noe further in this bufines of divorce whatfoeuer he had faid to him [2] before, but rather to arme and prepare himfelf againft thefe horrible herefies dayly entring into this realm, left by ouermuch negligence in repreffing them at the firft he fhould indaunger himfelfe and his whole realme fo farre, that at laft the foare might be growne vncurable, wherof he fhewed the example to be yet frefh in memorie in the realmes of Boheme and Hungarie. Many other lyke wordes he vttered to that effecte, wherin his repentance largely appeared. But to returne to our matter, the Cardinall fearing nowe left the kinge in whom he perceived the luftines of youth to vade and decaie, might foone waxe

---

[1] Fol. 36.   [2] Fol. 36, back.

wearye and repent himfelf of that wanton trade of lyfe, hitherto fpent for a great part in paftime and foolifh pleafure, wherby he might at laft, by the good queenes perfwafion (whom he knewe to beare him no great good favour) fall to ftraighter looking to the government of things then he had before done, and fo at lenge require accoumpt of his doinges : and being offended (as before is faid) at the Emperour and therby made on the french kings part, thought beft now to devife fome meane how to prevent this daunger, left by lyngring too longe, he might be difapointed of that he fo defired and erneftly affected to enioye. Now what the caufe was of this the [1]Cardinalls vniuft and malicious grudge againft this noble Queene, it fhall not be impertinent to our purpofe here by the waie to ope vnto you : and therfore you muft vnderftand, that at fuch time as it chaunced the Archbifhoprick of Toledo in Spaine to become voide, the Cardinall hearing therof, and being (as he was in deed) a man not only covetous and greedie of riches, but alfo of a marvelous and high afpiringe mind to honor, made meane ftraightway to the noble Emperour Charles the fifte to have and inioy that great dignitie, caufing the king to write erneftly to him in his behalf : But the wife Emperour, notinge the Cardinalls infatiable ambition and vanity, did altogether miflyke of it, and would in no wife condifcend to his requeft, wherat the Cardinall tooke such hartie difpleafure againft the Emperour that ever after he bare him in ftomacke.

Shortly after it fortuned the Sea Apoftolicke to become vacant by the death of Pope Leo the tenth, vnto which high prelacie the Cardinall ambitioufly afpired, and made great and fubtill meanes by helpe of divers frendes as well of King Henrie of England as of King Lewis of Fraunce, who for certaine purpofes travayled erneftly for him ; but therof he was likewife prevented and vtterly difapointed by the Emperour, who fo wrought with the Cardinalls in the conclave, that to that roome was elected Cardinall Hadrian, who fomtime before had bene his [2]fchoolemaister, and taught him in Loraine, and was called by the name of Hadrian the fixt, a man verie rare for his finguler vertue and learninge.

Thefe and fuch other things lying hott boylinge in the Car-

[1] Fol. 37.   [2] Fol. 37, back.

dinalls ftomacke againft the Emperour, he conceived at laft fuch malice againft him, that euer after he procured and labored by all his might to kindle variance and grudge betweene the king and him, cauling the kinge to ioyne in more affured amitie then he was wont with the kinge of Fraunce, whom he knewe to favour Themperour nothing at all. And yet not only content to maligne and envie the Emperour alone, he alfo fought by all the meanes he coulde to annoy and difpleafe his freindes and kindred for his fake. Amonge which the vertuous ladie Queene Catherin his Aunte was one, whom for her nephewes fake he agreeved and hurt many waies, but fpecially by raylinge this fecrett matter of difcorde between the kinge and her, wherby he might the rather bringe her in fome miflykinge of the kinge, and therwithall diminifhe the auncient and fure frendfhipp fo longe continewed between this Realme and the noble howfe of Burgundie; and fo treating with the kinge on a [1]time of fundrie matters, he brake at laft with him of his lacke of yffue male to fucceed him in the Crown of England, which he tooke to be the beft meane to enter fome fufpition into the kings head, for the maryage of his brothers wife. Saying vnto him that yt was a thinge much fpoken of, as well in forrain nations as here at home in his owne realme, and therfore in confcience (as he faid) he could not but aduertyfe him therof, for the love and duty he bare towards him, to the intent he might now confider of it, and inquire further. The kinge being at the firft moved and greatly difmaide at this ftrange motion, looking erneftly at the Cardinall for a good fpace, faid at the laft to him: "whie my lord, you know this mariage was greatly difcuffed in the beginninge amonge many learned men, and being by them at laft agreed for good and lawfull, it was after confirmed and difpenfed by the Pope himfelf, and therfore, good father, take heed what you do in this great and waightie matter," and fo immediatly vpon that motion departed a funder. But after that time, what by prick of his confcience, and what by the fleight of the Cardinall, he was as eafily taken as a fifh is with a hooke, for at the Cardinalls next comminge to him (which was within two or three daies after) he began to difcuffe with him the validitie of his maryage for a good

[1] Fol. 38.

ſpace together. The Cardinall having obtayned ſomwhat of that he
deſired, [1] and being now much more imbouldened then he was at t*h*e
firſt rehearſed the matter more fully, and at length wiſhing the
kinge to conferre with his ghoſtly father, which was then Doctor
John Longland, Biſhopp of Lincolne, a man verie timerous, and
loath to ſaie or doe anythinge *tha*t might any waies offend the kinge
or the Cardinall. Now what conference had bene betweene the
Cardinall and the byſhopp of Lincolne, I will not recite all that I
have heard. But by verie good and credible perſons it hath bene
reported, that the Cardinall ſtood in feare of a blind prophecie.
That a woman ſhould be his confuſion, which he coniectured to be
this good queen Catherin; for that he was alwaies french and
enemie to the Emperou*r* and his blood. Wherfore he perſwaded the
ſaid Biſhopp of Lincolne, that when the kinge ſhould deale with
him about any ſcruple of his maryage with his wife queen Catherin,
he ſhould in any wiſe further t*h*e ſame as much as in him laie, and
make it a matter of great conſcience to Cohabit with her, being not
his lawfull wife. The Biſhopp not forgetfull of his leſſon, when
ſhortly after the king had opened the matter to him, he ſtraight
waies adviſed him to conſulte further with ſome other learned
Biſhopps and Divines, for the better ſatiſfaccion of his [2] conſcience,
even in ſuch manne*r* as the Cardinall had inſtructed him, whervpon
the kinge vſinge againe the adviſe of the Cardinall, called many
other of the byſhopps toe debate the Cauſe, at the Cardinalls houſe
in Weſtm*inſ*ter. To this Counſell (amonge others) this worthie
Biſhopp of Rocheſter was ſpecially called, and there deſired to
ſpeake his minde frankly and freely: who without feare or reſpect
of the kinge, the Cardinall or any other man, ſhewed that there was
no cauſe at all of any queſtion, ſeeing t*h*e maryage betweene the king
and the Queene was good and lawfull from the beginninge; and therfore (ſaid he) it is rather neceſſarie to remove this ſcruple out of t*h*e
kings breſt as ſpedily as may be. And thus in concluſion, he refelled [3]
and fully anſwered manie reaſons that were there made by waie of
argument to the great ſatiſfaccion (as it ſeemed) of moſt of the
byſhops there aſſembled. When this matter was reported to the

[1] Fol. 38, back.   [2] Fol. 39.   [3] Harleian 7049, replyed.

king by *the* Cardinall, the kinge, who alreadie (as it after appeared by the fequell of the whole bufines) wifhed nothing more then to heare of a divorce, perceived that all did and was moſt lyke to fticke in my lord of Rocheſter, wherfore confultinge againe with the Cardinall what waie were beft to vfe to bringe him to favoure his defire, it was advifed by my lord Cardinall that the king fhould call vnto him my lord of Rocheſter, and by fair meanes worke him to incline to [1] his minde: wherfore the kinge, on a daie, fent to him and he came, the kinge vfinge him verie curteouflye gave him many reue*r*end and good wordes, and at laſt tooke him into the longe gallerie at Weſtm*inſter*; and there walking with him a while, after diue*rs* wordes of great praiſe geven him for his worthie learninge and vertue, he at laſt brake with him of this matter in the p*re*fence of the Dukes of Norff*olk* & Suff*olk*, and certaine of the Biſhopps, alleadginge there how fore his confcience was tormented, and how for *tha*t caufe he had fecretly confulted with his ghoftly father and diue*rs* other learned men, by whom he was not yet fatiffyed, and therfore faid that vpon fpeciall confidence in his great learninge, he had now made choife of him to vfe his advife above all others, praying him to declare his opinion freely, fo as with the hearing therof he might fufficiently be inftructed in his confcience, and remaine no longer in this fcruple, wherwith he was fo much vnquieted. My lord of Rocheſter hearinge all this Cafe proponed by the kinge, never ftucke longe in anfwering the matter, which he both [2] knew and thought to be good and true; but falling ſtraight waies upon his knees offered to fpeake to the kinge, but the king i*m*mediatly lyfted him vp againe with his owne hands and blamed him for fo doinge. Then ſpake this learned p*re*late, with a reue*r*end gravitie, after this or the lyke forte. " I befeech yo*ur* grace in gods name to be of good cheere, and no further to difmay yo*ur* felf with this matter, nether to vnquyet or trooble yo*ur* confcience for the fame, for " (faid he) " there is no heed to be taken to thefe men that account themfelves fo wife and arrogate to themfelves more cunninge & knowledge in divinitie then had all the learned fathers and divines, both of Spaine and alfo of this yo*ur* realme in yo*ur* late fathers time, nether yet fo

[1] Fol. 39, back.   [2] Fol. 40.

much credit to be geven vnto them as is to the Sea Apoftolicke, by whofe authoritie this maryage was confirmed, difpenfed, and approved for good and lawfull. Truly, truly" (faid he), "my foueraigne lord and kinge, you maie well and iuftly ought to make confcience of cafting any fcruple or doubt of this fo cleere and waightie a matter in bringing it by any meanes into queftion, and therefore by my advife and counfell you fhall with all fpeed put all fuch thought out of your minde; and as for any perill or daunger that to your foul maie infewe therby, I am not affraid in gevinge you this counfell to take vpon my owne foul all the damage, and will not refufe to anfwere againft all men in your behalf, ether privately or openly, that can any thing obiect againft [1]this matter, nothing doubtinge but there are many right worthie and learned perfons within this your realme, that be of this mind with me, and thinkes it a verie perrilous and vnfeemly thinge, that any Divorce fhould be fpoken of; vnto which fide I rather wifh your grace to hearken then to the other. And what color or fhewe they may feeme to have in this their motions to your highnes, yet god forbidd that your maieftie vpon fo fmall a foundacion fhould foe eafilie incline your felf to hearken to any perfon living in fo waightie a Cafe, paffed and eftablifhed by fo great an authoritie as the Sea Apoftolick." Thefe and diuers other lyke wordes he there vttered to the kinge which might have fatiffied his ficke minde, had not he bene other wife perverfly bent, and therfore all was in vaine; for the king (whether vpon remorfe of confcience, in deed, or feduced with ane other affection, I know not) alienated himfelf daily more and more from the company of the good queene, his wiffe, refufing to heare or geve care to all good counfell geven him by this good father & other learned men to the contrary, and fo for that time my lord of Rochefter departed from the kinge, who from that day forward never loked on him with merry countenaunce, as the good bifhop did wel perceive, for that his grudge daily increafed towards him.

[2]Whiles thefe things were thus in doinge it came to paffe that the king was fallen in love with a yong gentlewoman in the Court wayting on the Queene, called Miftris Ann Bollen, daughter of S.

[1] Fol. 40, back.   [2] Fol. 41.

Thomas Bollen, knight, who after, for his daughters fake, was promoted to many high honors and dignities. This Miſtriſs Ann had fomtime before that bene brought vp in the Court of Fraunce with the ladie marie, the french queene, that was fifter to kinge Henrie & fomtime wife to king Lewis the XIIth; where fhe learned much Courtly fafhion and manners, ftraunge and daintie in the Englifh Court, wherin fhe farr furpaffed other ladies, her companions, which fo inflamed the kings minde, that in the end he tooke her into his fecrett and deepe favour, and fo continewed many daies towards her, fhe knowing yet nothinge therof. But the flame at length burned fo farr within him that he began not only to fpeake of his forethought divorfe with Queene Catherin, but alfo of a new maryage with Miſtris Ann Bollen, wherin is to be noted the iuſt and fecret workinge of Almightie God; for although the Cardinall (to fatiffie his ambitious humor in eftablifhing that thinge which he fomwhat doubted) had wrought this variaunce between the king and the good queen, it fell out cleane contrarie to his expectacion, for it was nothing his meaninge the king fhould incline his minde to a new marriage this way, but rather els where, as he [1] had devifed, wherfore after Miſtris Ann had once knowledge of the kings fecrett good will towards her, and of the Cardinalls contrarie working to withftand the fame, fhe fo ordered the matter that in fhort fpace fhe wrought the Cardinalls vtter confufion, for now began the matter to worke apace, and that to be now ernestly and openly called vpon, which hitherto was but fecretly handled in Counfells and Convocacions of Bifhopps and other learned Divines. The kinge, I fay, began to open himfelf more fully then he had yet done, and for that purpofe were at my lord Cardinalls howfe at Weftminſter, affembled many notable and famous Clerkes, not only of both the vniuerfities of Cambridge and Oxford, but alfo of diuers Cathedrall Churches & religious howfes of this realme. There was this the kings matter debated, argued, and confulted the fpace of many daies, that it was a wonderfull thing to heare, but yet all fell not out fo cleere for the king as it was expected; for by the opinion of the greateſt number, the caufe was to hard and of to great importance for them to decide, and

[1] Fol. 41, back.

therefore the fathers departed without any refolucion. Howbeit diuers of the byfhops were of minde that the king fhould fend his Oratɔrs to fundrie vniuerfities, afwell abroad in Chriftendome as to the two vniuerfities at home, to haue his caufe difcuffed fubftantially amonge them, and the definicion therof to bringe with them in wrytinge vnder their common feales, [1] which was done accordingly to the kings great coft & charges; for yt was well knowne that thefe feales were obtained by corruption of money, and not by any free graunt or confent; neuertheles, great ioy was made for obtayninge therof, and the Orators were highly rewarded at their returne for their great laboures and travells, fome with Bifhoprickes, and fome otherwife farr beyond their merittes and defervings. Notwith-ftanding, the matter proceeded a pace, and thefe Inftrumentes thus obtayned vnder the vniuerfities feales were all delivered into the Cardinalls handes, who immediatly fent for all the Bifhops, and fell to counfultacion once againe, but all to litle purpofe; for ther the conclufion was, that although the vniuerfities had geven out thefe fenfures vnder their feales, yet was the caufe to great for them to define of themfelves, and therfore not to be further dealt in by them without the authoritie of the Sea Apoftolick; wherfore yt was agreed that the kinge fhould fend to Rome certaine Orators with the feales of thefe Vniuerfities, to treate with the Pope for his confirmacion. According to which refolucion the Ambaffadors were fpeedily dispatched to the Popes holinefs, which then was Clement the VIIth. The Ambaffadors names were these: Doctor Stephen Gardiner, the kings Secretarie; Sir Thomas Bryan, knight, one of the gentlemen of the kings privie chamber; Sir Gregorie de Caffales, an Italian; and Maister [2] Peter Vanus, a Venetian. Thefe Ambaffadors being arrived at Rome, after they had propounded the caufe of their comminge, and a while refted themfelves, the matter fell fpeedily in hand. Then wanted no pofting of letters betweene the kinge and the ambaffadors, inftructing them from time to time how to deale with the Pope, that this bufines might be brought about. Lykewife the Cardinall omitted noe time or occafion by his letters to fett forward the fame. But (god fo orderinge the matter) the Ambaffadors were

[1] Fol. 42.   [2] Fol. 42, back.

not half fo haftie in demaundinge, but the Pope was as flow in grauntinge, and much the flower, by reafon of his ficknes, being at that time fo fore pained with *th*e goute that there was doubt of his lyfe. Wherfore after knowledge come once to the kinge and the Cardinall, then letters went thicke and threefould to the Orators, willinge them to call more erneftly vpon him for his definitive anfwere, thinking now by reafon of the great paine he continevally felt of his infirmitie, he would the rather be ridd of their callinge, and fo end the matter, according to their demaund. further, they had inftrucc*i*on from the king and the Cardinall in their letters, that in cafe the Pope chanced to die at this p*r*efent, *tha*t then they fhould by all meanes they could devife fome way how the Cardinall of Yorke might be elected to fucceed in [1]the place, and for furtherance therof to deale with certaine Cardinalls, promifinge them in the kings name golden mountaines and filver rivers to geve their fuffrages with him. And in cafe they would not by this meanes bringe their purpofes to paffe, but that the Cardinalls in *th*e Conclave would needes chufe into the place fome fuch as p*er*haps would not further *th*e kinges entent, then to take vp a fome of money vpon the kings creditt, and therewithall to raife a power or p*r*efidie of men (as by the kings letters and the Cardinalls it is tearmed), and taking with them fuch Cardinalls as might be brought to favour their purpofe, to depart out of the Cittie into fome out place not farr of, and there to make a fchifme in election of the Cardinall of Yorke to the Papacie. But (lauded be god) all fell out otherwife then was then mente; for the Pope recovered health, & after lived to finifh all bufines, though in deed cleane otherwife then the kinge expected, as after fhall be declared. wherfore feeing none of thefe wais would fpeed, and finding that the Pope would make no fuch haft in fatiffying the kings defire as the Orators required, yt was at laft requefted that it might pleafe his holynes to fend a Legate into England, geving him full authoritie to heare the Cafe debated there, and finally to geve fentence according to right and equitie. After *th*e expences of many [2]daies the Pope was at laft contented (with much adoe) to agree to that requeft; and to this affaire he appointed Law-

[1] Fol. 43. [2] Fol. 43, back.

rence Campagius, a Cardinall of the Church of Rome, intituled : fancte
Mariæ trans Tiberim : a man verie well learned, and of great corrage
and magnanimitie, to whom the king, about ten yeres afore, had
geven the Bifhoprick of Bathe at his being in England about another
matter. The Ambaffadors beinge returned with this conclufion there
refted no more then but to prepare for the legates comminge ; who
(after longe expectacion and many wearie iorneys) arived at laft in
England, and cominge to london was lodged at Bath place, fometime his owne howfe : But before his arival it was thought verie
neceffary by fuch as favored the kings purpofe, that the Cardinall of
Yorke fhould be ioyned in Commiffion with him. Whervpon fuch
fpeedie order was taken that before Campagius came to Callis, a new
Commiffion was brought him from the Pope, wherin the Cardinall
of Yorke and he were made ioynt Commiffioners together. And
becaufe the Pope vnderftood that king Henry defired nothing more
then a full & fpeedie expedition of this matter, and was verie im-
patient of longe tractinge[1] of time in tryall therof, [2]the more to put
the king in hope of readie iuftice (if the equitie of his caufe fo
required), he made (as I have heard fay) a Bull of fentence to be
written readie, wherin the maryage was vtterly fruftrat and made
void ; and this Bull he deliuered verie fecretly to Cardinall Campeius after his departure, willing and charging him, neuertheles, that
after the Bull once fhowed to the kinge and the Cardinall, he fhould
after keepe it clofe from all others, and in no wyfe to publifh the fame
till fuch time as he had received a new authoritie and commaundment from him ; no although he fawe and had proof of fufficient
matter fo to geve fentence. And this the Pope did only to the
intent that the kinge fhould the more quietly be content to have all
tryed in dew forme and order of lawe, although it were the longer in
doinge. When the two Cardinalls were mett and had commoned a
feafon of their bufines, they firft tooke order for the open readinge
and declaringe of their commiffion. Then a place was affigned where
it fhould be done, and that was at the Dominicke Freers in London,
and the king with the queene his wife fhould be lodged at a place
now called Bridewell, ftanding hard by. Then ftood readie the

[1] treatinge, Harleian 7049.   [2] Fol. 44.

Counfellors learned as well on the kings part as on the queens; for the kinge (becaufe he would feeme indifferent) willed the queen to chufe her counfell: which although of her felf fhe would chufe none at all, becaufe fhe fufpected the indifferencie of the kings owne fubiectes towardes her being in his owne dominion and Realme, yet for fafhion fake [1] were affigned vnto her diuers learned men; that is to fay of Divines. This excellent man of whom we intreate, John Fyfher, Bifhopp of Rochefter; Henrie Standifh, byfhopp of Saint Affaphe; Thomas Abell, Richarde Fetherftone, Edward Powell, and Robert Ridley, all Doctors of Divinitie. And of Civillians and Cannouiftes were there, William Warham, Archbifhopp of Canterberie; Cuthbert Tunftall, byfhop of London; Nicholas Weft, byfhopp of Elye; and John Clarke, byfhopp of Bathe, becaufe Cardinall Campeius was then tranflated to the Sea of Salefburie: fhe had alfo other profound Clerkes, afwell divines as lawyers. On the kings part were alfo another lyke number of learned doctors. Then peace and filence was proclaymed, and the Commiffion was read; that being done, this our learned bifhopp offered vp to the Legates a booke which he had compyled in defence of the maryage, and therwith made a learned and grave Oration vnto them, defyring them to take good heede what they did in this waightie Cafe, putting them in minde of fundrie manifold daungers that were lykely to enfewe, not only to this Realme, but alfo to the whole ftate of Chriftendome, by bringing in queftion the validitie or invaliditie of this maryage, being in deed a matter fo plaine, as there was no doubt therin at all. After that his oration was ended, the kinge was called [2] by name, and anfwered (here). Then was the queen called, who made no anfwere, but rofe immediatly out of her chair, and comminge aboute by the Courte, fhe kneeled down to the kinge openly in fight of the Legates and all the Court, & fpake in effect thefe wordes, fome in broken englifh, and fome in french. "Sir" (quoth fhe), "I befeech you doe iuftice and right and take fome pittie vpon me, for I am a fimple woman and a ftranger, borne out of your dominions, havinge here no indifferent counfell, and leffe affurance of frendfhip. Alas, Sir, what have I offended you, or what occafion of difpleafure have I

---

[1] Fol. 44, back.   [2] Fol. 45.

geven you, that fhould goe about to put me from you after this fort.
I take god to my iudge I have bene to you a trewe and humble wife
ever conformable to your will and pleafure. I neuer contraried or
gainfaid you therin, but alwaies contented my felf with all things
wherin you had delight and pleafure, whether yt were litle or much,
without grudge or countenance of difcontentacion. I loved for your
fake all them that you loved, whether I had caufe or not, or whether
they were my frendes or foes; I have bene your wife this twentie
yeres, and you have had by me diuers children, and when you tooke
me at the firft (I take god to my iudge) I was a verie maide, and
whether it be trewe or noe I put it to your confcience. [1] Now if
there be any iuft caufe that you alleadge againft me, ether of dif-
honeftie or other matter, wherby you may put me from you, I am
content to depart with fhame and rebuke; but yf there be none,
then, I pray you, let me have iuftice at your hands. The kinge, your
father, was in his time of fuch an excellent witt that he was accounted of many men for his wifdome a fecond Solomon. And king
Ferdinando, my father, was reckoned to be one of the wyfeft princes
that raygned in Spaine many yeres before his daies. Thefe being
both fo wife princes, it is not to be doubted but they had gathered
vnto them as wife Counfellors of euery realme as by their wifdomes
they thought meet: And as I take yt, there were in thofe daies as
wyfe and well learned in both realmes as be now in thefe daies, who
thought at that time the marryage between you and me to be good
and lawfull. But of all this bufines I may thanke you, my lord
Cardinall of Yorke, who having longe fought to make this diffention
between my lord the kinge and me, becaufe I have fo ofte found
falt with your pompe and vanitie and afpiring mind. Howbeit, this
your malice againft me proceedeth not from you as in refpect of my
felf aloane, but your cheefe difpleafure is againft my [2] Nephewe the
Emperor, for that at his handes you were firft repelled from the
Bifhoppricke of Toledo, which greedily you defired; and after that
were by his meanes kept from the cheefe and high Bifhopprick
of Rome, whervnto moft ambitioufly you afpired: wherat being
fore offended, and yet not able to revenge your quarrell on him, you

[1] Fol. 45, back.   [2] Fol. 46.

have now raifed this quarrell againft me, his poore Aunte, thinking therby to eafe your cruell minde, for the which god forgeve you and amend you. It is therfore a wonder to heare what newe inventions are nowe devifed againft me that neuer entended but honeftly. And now to caufe me to ftand to the order and iudgment of this Court, ye fhould (faid fhe to the kinge) do me much wronge, as feemeth to me, feeinge one of the iudges is partiall againft me, and hath fought meanes to raife this difpleafure betweene you and me. And further, yf I fhould agree to ftande to the iudgment of this courte ye may condemne me for lacke of anfwere, havinge noe counfell but fuch as you have affigned me, and thofe ye may well confider cannot be indifferent on my part, feeinge they be your owne fubiectes and fuch as you have taken & chofen out of your owne counfell, whervnto they are privie and dare not difclofe your will and intent. Therfore [1]I refufe here to ftand to the order of this Courte, and doe appeale to the Sea Apoftolicke before our holy father the Pope, humbly befeechinge you in the way of charitie to fpare me till I may further vnderftand what waye my frendes in Spaine will advife me to take; And yf you will not this doe, then your pleafure be fulfilled." And with that fhe rofe vp, and makinge a lowe Curtefie to the kinge departed, leavinge there many a weeping eye & forrowfull hart, that heard her lamentable wordes. Amongft whom this worthie Bifhop of Rochefter (as one that knewe moft of the equitie of the caufe) was not able to refraine from teares: which open fight caufed many other to have the more compaffion of the good queenes caufe.

As foone as the queen was vp, it was fuppofed that fhe would have returned to her place from whence fhe came, but fhe departed ftraight out of the Court, and would in no wife returne, faying to fuch as were about her, that fhe would no longer tarrye, for the Court was not indifferent for her; and fo fhe departed for that time, and would neuer after appeare in open cort.

[2]The kinge, perceivinge that fhe was thus gone, & confidering well on the wordes fhe had there fpoken, faid to the audience thus in effect. / 'Forafmuch as the queene is now gone, I will in her

[1] Fol. 46, back.   [2] Fol. 47.

abfence declare vnto you all, That fhe hath bene to me as trewe, as obedient, and as conformable a wife as I could wifh or defire; fhe hath all the vertuous quallities *that* ought to be in a woman of her dignitie, or any other, yea, though fhe were of bafer ftate. She is alfo a noble woman borne, as her noble condici*o*ns will well declare, and the fpeciall caufe that moved me in this matter was a certaine fcruple, *that* prickt my co*n*fcience. Whether my daughter Marie fhould be legittimate or no, in refpect of this marryage with this woman being fomtimes my brothers wife: which thinge once conceived in the fecrett*es* of my breft, by a certain occafion geven me when time was, ingendred fuch a fcrupilous doubt in me, that my mind was incontinently accombred, vexed, and difquyeted, wherby I miftrufted my felfe to be greatly in the daunger of gods indignaci*o*n, which appeared to me (as to me feemed the rather), for that he fent vs no iffue male, and that all fuch iffues as fhe had by me dyed incontinently after [1] they came into this world: So that I doubted *th*e great difpleafure of Almightie god in that behalf. Thus my confcience, beinge toffed too and froe with the waves of continewall vnquietnes, and almoft in difpaire to haue any other yffue then I had alreadie by this ladie, it behooved me further to confider the ftate of this Realme, and the daunger it ftood in for lacke of a prince to fucceed me. And therfore, I thought it good in releafe of this mightie burthen of my confcience, and the quiet ftate of this noble realme, to attempt the lawe therin, whether I might lawfully take an other wife, by whom god may fend me yffue, in cafe this, my firft marryage, were not good. And this is the only caufe I have fought thus farr, and not for any difpleafure or diflykinge of the queens perfon or age, with whom I could be as well content to continewe (yf our marryage maie ftand with *the* lawes of god) as with any woman alive. And in this point confifteth all the doubt that we goe about to trie, by the learninge, wifdome, & iudgment*es* of you, my lordes, the prelat*es* and paftors of this our realme, now here affembled for that purpofe: to whofe confcience and learninge I have committed *the* charge therof, and according to that will I be content (god willinge) to fubmitt myfelf with obedience. And that [2] I ment

[1] Fol. 47, back.   [2] Fol. 48.

not to wade in fo waightie a matter of my felf without the opinion
and iudgment of you, my lor*des* fpirituall, it may well appeare in
this, that fhortly after the comminge of this fcruple into my head, I
moved it to you, my lord of Lincolne, then my ghoftly father. And
forafmuch as yo*ur* felf were then in fome doubte, you advifed me to
afke the Counfell of the reft of my Lordes the Bifhops; whervpon
I moved you, my lord of Canterburie, firft to haue yo*ur* licence (in as
much as you were metropolitane) to put this matter in queftion; and
fo I did of all you, my lordes, to which you all graunted under yo*ur*
feales, and that I have here to be fhewed.' 'That is trew, yf yt
pleafe yo*ur* grace,' quoth my lord of Canterburie, ' and I doubt not
but my bretheren here will acknowledge the fame.' /

Then my lord of Rochefter, knowinge the cleernes of his owne
confcience, and perceivinge the dooble dealinge in this matter, was
forced for difcharge of his owne credit and truth, to breake a litle
fquare, and faid to my lord of Canterburie, ' No, no, my lord, not foe.
Vnder yo*ur* favour all the bifhopps were not fo farre agreed, for to
that inftrument you have nether my hand nor feale.' 'Noe, ah,'
(quoth the kinge,) & therwith lookinge vpon my lord of Rochefter
with a frowninge [1] countenance, faid, 'looke here, Is not this yo*ur*
hand and yo*ur* feale?' and fhewed him the Inftrument with feales.
' No, for footh,' quoth the Bifhop. ' How faie you to that?' faid
the kinge to my lorde of Canterburie. ' S*ir*,' faid he, ' it is his hand
and his feale.' ' No, my lord,' quoth the Bif*h*op of Rochefter againe.
' Indeed, you were often in hand with me for my hand and my
feale, as other of my lords have done; but then I eue*r* faid to you,
I would in no wife confent to any fuch Acte, for it was much
againft my confcience to have this matter fo much as once called in
queftion, and therfore my hand and feale fhould neue*r* be put
to any fuch inftrument, god willinge, with more communicac*ion*
between vs in that bufines, yf you remember.' ' Indeed,' quoth my
lo*rd* of Canterburie, ' Trew it is that fuch wordes you had with me,
but after our talke ended, you were at laft refolved and content that
I fhold fubfcribe yo*ur* name, and put to yo*ur* feale, and you would
allowe *th*e fame as yf it had bene done by yo*ur* felf.' Then my lord

[1] Fol. 48, back.

of Rochefter, feeinge himfelf fo iniuftly charged by the Bifhop of
Canterburie, faid vnto him openly againe, 'No, my lord, by your
favour and licence, all this you have faid of me is vntrewe'; and
with [1]that ment to have faid more, but that the king ftopping him,
faid, 'Well, well, my lord of Rochefter, it maketh noe great matter;
we will not ftand with you in argument about this bufines, for you
are but one man amonge *th*e reft, if the worft fall.' and fo for that
time all was ended.

Shortly after, an other daie of fittinge was appointed, where they
two Cardinalls were prefent, at which time the Counfell on both
fides were there readie to anfwer. There was much matter proponed
by the Counfell on the kings parte to prove the maryage not lawfull
from the begininge, becaufe of the carnall copulac*i*on had betweene
prince Arthur and the queene. This matter being vehemently
vrged, many reafons and fimilitudes were alleadged to prove the
carnall copulac*i*on, but, being againe negatively anfwered by the
counfell of the queenes fide, all feemed to reft vpon proof, which was
verie hard and almoft vnpoffible to be tryed. But my lord of
Rochefter faid, that the truth of this marryage was plaine ynough to
be proved good and lawfull from the begininge, whether there were
carnall knowledge betweene the parties or noe; for the Cafe (he
faid) was thoroughly fcanned and debated in the begininge by
many great learned Divines and lawiers, wherof [2]himfelf remembred
the time, and was not altogether ignorant of the manne*r* of dealinge
therin. And being after ratifyed and approved by authoritie of the
Sea Apoftolicke, fo amply and fo largely, he thought yt a hard
matter to call it now againe in queftion before any other Iudge.
Then fpake doctor Ridley (who was a man of verie litle and fmall
pe*r*fonage / but high of corrage and profound in learninge), and he
faid to my lord Cardinall, That it was a great fhame and difhonor to
this honorable p*r*efence, that any fuch p*r*efumptious fimilitudes &
Coniectures fhould be fo openly alleadged: for they be deteftable to
be rehearfed. 'What!' (quoth my lord Cardinall), 'domine doctor,
magis reuerenter.' 'No, no, my lor*d*,' quoth he, 'there belongeth no
reue*r*ence to be geven at all, for an vnreuerent matter would be

[1] Fol. 49.   [2] Fol. 49, back.

vnreverently anſwered.' Againſt that Court daie the Biſhop of London, Cuthbert Tunſtall, had framed and written a verie learned treatiſe in defence of the queenes maryage, which he deliuered before to Cardinall Campeius, to be read at the daie: but the king, fearinge him much (as he was indeed a very famous learned man), made ſuch ſpeedie order with him, that he was of [1] purpoſe ſent away ambaſſador into Scotland about a matter of ſmall importance, and appeared not in the Court the ſecond fittinge, by reaſon wherof the booke was not reade at all: Neuertheles, Cardinall Campeius called for him, and wiſhed to heare him ſpeake, for he ſaid in latine: Cum Tonſtallum lego videor mihi ipſum vſpiam audire. Thus, proceedinge from daie to daie, the Legates ſtill ſate at their accuſtomed place, but all matters of queſtion were cleane laid aſide, ſeeing the queen had appealled, and they now inquired only of ſuch things as belonged to inſtruccion of the cauſe, and informacion to be geven to the Popes holines. / But the Biſhopp of Elie, beinge one of the queenes counſell, and one that miſtruſted the Cardinall of Yorkes iuſt and trewe dealinge with her, openly declared in his wrytinge that he marveled what my lordes the legates ment, to heare or hould any further plea of this matter, ſeeing the queen had made her appeale to a higher Judge then they. The matter being come to this concluſion the kinge was cleane diſapointed, and driven now to ſeeke a new waie. Wherfore he ſent for the Cardinall of Yorke to come vnto him, and gave vnto him a greate charge to goe with the other Cardinall his fellowe to the queen, and by their wiſdomes to perſwade with her to geue ouer her appeall, and to ſtand to the iudgment of [2] this Court, or els to ſurrender the matter into his handes, which ſhould be much better and more honorable for both parties than to ſtand to open tryall in the Court of Rome. / The Cardinall, to ſatiſfie the kings pleaſure, did accordinge to his commaundment, but all in vaine, for the queen ſtood verie ſtifly to her appeale, and could by no meanes be altered from that minde, for any thinge the Cardinall of Yorke could ſaie or doe, who was much more erneſt with her then the other Cardinall was, ſhe alleadginge ſtill for her ſelf, her ſimplicitie and vnablenes to anſwere in ſo waightie a matter, beinge but a woman, and cleane

[1] Fol. 50.   [2] Fol. 50, back.

CARDINAL CAMPEIUS REFUSES TO PRONOUNCE JUDGMENT. 65

deſtitute of frendes or counſell here within the kings realme, for (thinke you) ſaid ſhe, that any of the kings ſubiectes will adventure themſelves to incurre his diſpleaſure for my cauſe? No, no: And therefore I pray you beare with me, a poore woman deſtitute of frendſhip, and lett me have your charitable counſell what is beſt for me to doe, ſo as all may be ended to the glorie of god and ſatiſfaccion of the kings maieſtie and me. This communicacion ended, they returned to the kinge and made relation of her talke. /

This ſtrange Caſe proceedinge thus from day to day & court to Court, the kinge at laſt grewe wearie and [1] vrged the Cardinalls to a finall daie of ſentence, at which time the kinge came thither, and was openly ſett in his Chayre to heare the iudgment, where all their proceedings and actes were openly read in latine: That done the kinges Counſell called for iudgment: with that ſaid Cardinall Campeius in latin, "No, not ſo, I will geve no ſentence till I have made relation vnto the Pope of all our doings, whoſe commandment I will obſerve in this Caſe; the matter is to high for vs to define haſtely, confidering the highnes of the perſons and the doubtfull argumentes alleadged, remembringe alſo whoſe commiſſioners we be, and vnder whoſe authoritie we ſitt, it were (me thinketh) good reaſon we ſhould make our cheef head of counſell therwith before we proceede to ſentence definitive. I come not hither to pleaſe, for favour, meede, or dreed of any perſon alive, be he kinge or ſubiect, neither have I ſuch reſpect to the perſon, that I will offend my conſcience or diſpleaſe god. I am now an ould man, both weake and ſicklye, and daily looke for death'; and ſhould I nowe put my ſoul in daunger of gods diſpleaſure to my euerlaſtinge damnacion for the favour or feare of any prince in this worlde? My comminge hither is only to ſee [2] iuſtice miniſtred accordinge to my conſcience. And for aſmuch as I vnderſtand by the allegacions the matter to be verie doubtfull and alſo that the partie defendant will make no anſwere here, but doth rather appeale from vs, ſuppoſinge that we cannot be indifferent iudges for her, confideringe the kings high authoritie and dignitie within his owne realme, where ſhe thinketh we dare not doe her iuſtice, for feare of his diſpleaſure. Therfore to avoid all theſe

[1] Fol. 51.   [2] Fol. 51, back.

ambiguities I will not damne my foule for any prince or potentate alive. In confideration wherof I intend not to wade any further in this matter till I have the iuft opinion & affent of the Pope, and fuch other as be better feen in fuch doubtfull caufes of lawe then I am. Wherfore I do here adiourne this Court for this time, accordinge to the order of the Court of Rome, from whence our authoritie is derived, which yf we fhould tranfgreffe might be accounted in vs great follie and rafhnes, and redound to our difcredit and blame. And with that the Court was diffolved, and no more was euer done after that daie.

[1] The noble men about the kinge, feeinge all this bufines come to this conclufion, began to mutine and fpeake ill of the two Cardinalls, fpecially fuch as were flatterers & parafites about the kinge. In fo much as the Duke of Suffolke, Charles Brandon, whom the kinge hadd before highly advaunced from a bafe ftate to great honors and poffeffions, and alfo geven him his owne fifter in marriage, clapping his hands on the board, fware, by gods blood, that he found now the oulde faying was trewe: That Cardinalls did neuer good in England, and that he fpake with fuch a fpirit of vehemencie, and with fo clamarous a noyfe, that all men about him marveled what he mente; and wife men thought he durft not thus have faid, but that he knew the kings minde aforehande.

The kinge himfelf conceived lykewife greate indignacion and difpleafure, both againft the Cardinall of Yorke, and alfo the queenes counfell, for that he had lofte and fpente in vaine (as he thought) all this longe time, and grewe now fo wrathfull againft them that he detirmined in his minde neuer to ceafe till he was revenged on them all, as after it came [2] to paffe in deede, though greatly to all their merittes and euerlaftinge glorie, and his owne perpetuall ignominy and reproach; for of this braunch proceeded the death, not only of this holy and reuerend bifhop of whom we intreate, but alfo of that glorious man, Sir Thomas More, with many other worthie and famous prelates and lay men, wherof three, that were fometime of the queenes learned Counfell in this matter of divorfe, were put to moft cruell death in Smithfeild, all in one daie, which was alfo ment

---

[1] Fol. 52. [2] Fol. 52, back.

to the reft had it not bene that death by great forrow and greefe fhortned fome of their daies, and prevented the kings purpofe, as happened to the byfhop of Eelye and Doctor Rydley. And fome other not being of fuch fortitude as the reft were, yelded them felves for feare to the kings will and pleafure, leaving the queene (as they call yt) in plaine feilde. Amonge which the bifhop of Canterburie was one who moft deceived her and many moe.

Cardinall Campeius perceiving *the* kinge now fallen into this furie, and further feeing that there was no more to be done by him nor his fellowe (the queene havinge made her appeale), he thought it therefore beft to be fhortly gone, and fo taking his [1] leave of the kinge departed towards Rome, after he had tarried in England about this bufinefs nighe the fpace of one yere. He was no fooner gone, but a rumor rofe (I wott not by what meanes) that he had carried with him a greate heap of treafure of the other Cardinalls, who for fear of the kings difpleafure was fufpected lykely to flie out of the realme. Infomuch as he fent fpeedily after Cardinall Campeius certaine perfons, who ouertooke him at Callis, and there ftaid him till he was fearched verie narrowly, and when they had done all that could be done, they found about him fcant fo much money as would pay for his rydinge charges, and fo difmiffed him on his iorney greatly difcontented. Now although the color of this fearch was for the Cardinall of Yorkes treafure, yet in deed it was well knowne after to be done for an other purpofe; for the kinge thought to haue found about him the Inftrument (wherof we fpake lately before) deliuered vnto him by the Pope at his departure from Rome, wherin was contayned the fentence of Divorce: which if he might have found, no doubt but he would have made fome play therwith, whether *the* meaninge of the Pope had bene to have it publifhed or no. But he was for all that deceived of his purpofe, and all they that gave him Counfell to the fame.

[2] By this time the kings ire was fo fore kindled againft the whole Clergie, and fpecially againft this our holy Bifhop (whom he knewe to beare fuch a ftroake amonge them, that as longe as he was there nothinge could fucceed accordinge to his purpofe), that he began to

[1] Fol. 53.   [2] Fol. 53, back.

deuife newe lawes againft the right and patrimonye of the Church; for in the xxij[th] yere of his raigne he fommoned a parlement to begin at London the third daie of November, which was in the yere of our Lord god 1529. In this parlement the common howfe was fo parcially chofen, that the king had his will almoft in all things that himfelf lifted; for where in old time the king vfed to direct his brieffe or writ of parleament to euery Cittie, Borrough, and corporat towne within this Realme, that they amonge them fhould make election of two honeft, fitt, and fkilfull men of their owne number to come to this parleament; the fame order and forme of the Writt was now in this parleament obferued; but then with euery writte there came alfo a private letter from fome one or other of the kings Counfellors, requeftinge them to chufe the perfons nominated in their letters, who fearing their great authoritie, durft commonly chufe none other; fo that where in times paft, [1] the Common howfe was vfually furnifhed with grave and difcreet townes men, apparreled in comlie and fage furred gownes; now might you have feene in this parleament fewe others then royftinge courteours, feruingmen, parafites, and flatterers of all fortes highly apparelled in fhort clokes and fwordes, and as lightly furnifhed ether with learninge or honeftie, fo that when any thinge was moved againft the fpiritualtie or the libertie of the church, to that they harkned dilligently, geving ftraight their affentes in any thing that the king would require. Then were preferred in the common howfe, all the flaunderous bills againft the Clergie that might be devifed, complayning of their ydlenefs, their great wealth, and abufe in fpendinge of their revennews: wherof although fome bills were reiected in the higher howfe, yet many toke place. Amonge whiche one was, for abating of charges in the probate of Teftaments and wills: An other was for diminifhinge of mortuaries; Another againft pluralities of benefices and taking of Farmes by fpirituall men, which were all directly paffed by the common howfe in derogation and preiudice of the Church: but after they were brought to the higher howfe and there read, my lord of Rochefter ftepped vp amonge the other [2] lordes, and faid in effect as followeth: "My lordes, I pray you for gods

[1] Fol. 54.   [2] Fol. 54, back.

fake confider what bills are here daily preferred from the commons; what the fame may found in fome of your yeres I cannot tell, but in my yeres they found all to this effect. That our holy Mother the Churche beinge left vnto vs by the great liberallitie and dilligence of our forefathers, in moſt perfect & peaceable freedome, ſhall now by vs be brought into fervile thraldome, lyke to a bound maid, or rather by litle & litle to be cleane baniſhed and driven out of our confines and dwelling places; for els to what end ſhould all this importunate and iniurious petitions from the Commons tende? What ſtrange words be here vttered, not to be heard of any *Chriſ-tian* eares, and vnworthie to be fpoken in the hearing of *Chriſten* princes; For they faie *that* biſhops and their aſſociates, Abbots, prieſts, and other of *the* Clergie are vitious, ravenous, infatiable, ydle, cruell, and fo forth. What, are all of this fort? or is there any of theſe abuſes that the Clergie ſeeke not to extirpe & deſtroy? Be there not lawes alreadie provided againſt fuch and many moe diforders? Are not bookes full of them to be reade of fuch as lift to reade them, yf they were executed? But, my lordes, beware of your felves and your Countrey; nay, beware of the libertie of our [1] mother the Church. Luther, one of the moſt cruell enemies to the faith that ever was, is at hand, and the common people ſtudie for novelties, and with good will heare what can be faid in favour of hereſie. What fucceſſe is there to be hoped for in theſe attempts other then fuch as our neighboures have alreadie taſted, whoſe harmes may be a good warning to vs? Remember with your felves what theſe fects and diviſions have wrought amonge the Bohemians and Germans, who, befides an innumerable number of miſcheefes fallen amonge them, have almoſt loſt their auncient and catholyke faith: And what by the fnares of John Huffe, and after him Martin Lūther (whom they reuerence like a prophett), they have almoſt excluded them felves from the Vnitie of *Chriſtes* holy Church. Theſe men now amonge vs feeme to reprove the life and doings of the clergie; but after fuch a fort as they indevour to bringe them into contempt and hatred of the layetie, and fo finding falte with other mens manners whom they haue noe authoritie to correct, ommitt

[1] Fol. 55.

and forget their owne, which is far worfe & much more out of order then the other. But yf *th*e truth were knowne ye fhall find that they rather hunger and thirft after the riches and poffeffions of *th*e clergie ¹then after amendment of their faltes and abufes. And therefore it was not for nothing that this motion was lately made for the fmall Monafteries to be taken into the kings handes. Wherfore I will tell you (my lordes) playnly, what I thinke, except you refift manfully by yo*ur* authorities this violent heape of mifcheefe offered by the commons, ye fhall fhortly fee all obedience withdrawne, firft from *th*e clergie, and after yo*ur* felves, whervpon will infewe the vtter ruine and daunger of the Chriftian faith; and in place of it (that which is lykely to followe) the moft wicked and tyrannicall government of the Turke; for ye fhall finde that all thefe mifcheefs amonge them ryfeth throwgh lack of faith."

This fpeech beinge ended, although there were dive*rs* of the Clergie that lyked well therof, and fome of *th*e Layetie alfo, yet were there fome againe that feemed to miflyke the same only for flatterie & feare of *th*e king, in fo much as the Duke of N*o*rffol*k*e reproved him half merrily and half angerly, fayinge that many of thefe wordes might have bene miffed, adding further thefe wordes (ywis, my lord, it is many times feene that the greateft clerkes be not alwayes the wifeft men); ²but to that he anfwered as merrily againe, and faid that he could not remember any fooles in his time *tha*t had proved great clerkes. But when the commons heard of thefe wordes fpoken againft them, they ftraightwaie conceived fuch difpleafure againft my lord of Rochefter, that by the mouth of M*aifte*r Audley, their Speaker, they made a greevous complaint to the king of his wordes, fayinge, that it was a great difcredit to them all to be thus charged that they lacked faith, which in effect was all one to faie they were hereticks and infidells, and therfore defired the king that they might have fome remedie againft him. The kinge therfore to fatiffie them called my lord of Rochefter before him, and demaunded whie he fpake in that fort: And he anfwered againe that (being in counfell) he fpake his minde in defence and right of the Church, whom he fawe daily iniured and oppreffed amonge the common people, whofe

¹ Fol. 55, back.   ² Fol. 56.

office was not to deale with her, and therfore faid that he thought himfelf in confcience bound to defend her all that he might. The kinge neuertheles willed him to vfe his wordes temperatly. And fo the matter ended, much to the difcontentacion of M*aifte*r Audley and diuers others of the common howfe.

In the fame parlement was alfo a motion made (as ye have heard before), that the king had bene at [1]great charges and large expenfes in fuinge forth fundrie Inftrumentes towchinge the divorce betweene him and queene Catherine, which cheefly rofe (as was there faid) by the falfe and dooble dealinge of the Cardinall and the Clergie, and therfore reafon that it fhould be anfwered amonge them againe. And to fatiffie this matter withall, nothing was thought fo convenient as to recompence him in the Convocacion, by graunting vnto him all the fmall Abbays and Monafteries within this realme of the valewe of two hundred poundes, landes and vnder. This matter was hardly vrged and fett forth by many of the kings counfell, with all the tirrible fhewe that might be of the kings difpleafure, yf it were not graunted according to his requeft and demaund. Infomuch as diuers of the Convocacion, fearinge the kings greevous indignacion and crueltie, and thinking that their yelding in this matter would be a meane to ftopp all and fave the reft, were of minde to condifcend to that demaund. But the good father could neuer be brought to that opinion, but openly refifted it with all the force he could. And on a time faid amonge them, "My lordes, I praie you take good heed what you doe in haftie grauntinge to the kings demaund in this great matter. It is here required that we fhoulde [2]graunt vnto him the fmall Abbaies for the eafe of his charges; whervnto, yf we condifcend, it is lykely the great will be demaunded or it be longe after: And therfore confideringe the manner of this dealinge it putteth me in remembrance of a fable. Howe the Axe that lacked a handle came on a time to the wood, and making his moane to the great trees, how that for lack of a handle to worke withall he was faine to ftand ydle: he therfore defired of them to graunt him fome yonge fapling in the wood to make him one; they miftruftinge no gulle forth with graunted a

[1] Fol. 56, back.   [2] Fol. 57.

yong fmall tree, wherof he fhaped himfelf a handle, and being at laft a perfect axe in all points, he fell to worke, and fo labored in the wood, that in proceffe of time he left nether great tree nor fmall ftandinge. And fo, my lordes, yf ye graunt to the kinge the fmall Monafteries ye do but make him a handle, and fo geve him occafion to demaund the reft or it be longe after, wherof cannot but enfewe the difpleafure of Almightie god in that ye take vpon you to geve the things that is none of your owne." To this Counfell moft of the lordes in the Convocacion inclyned, and fo for that time all was reiected and no more faid as longe as this good father lived; but fhortly after his death the matter was revived and graunted to the kings firft will and pleafure.

[1] Now whileft thefe things were thus in handlinge, it chaunced this reuerend father to fall into a great daunger and perrill, wherby he efcaped verie narrowly with his life; for a certaine naughtye perfon, of a moft damnable and wicked difpofition, provided on a daie a quantitie of poifon, and came with the fame into my lord of Rochefters howfe to the Cooke, beinge of his acquaintance, between whom, after a few wordes had paffed, the Cooke offered him to drinke, and fo went to the buttrie to fetch him drinke: Then this vngodly perfon, having gotten a good oportunitie for his purpofe (while nobody was left within the Kitchin) threwe the poyfon into a paile of yeft, wherof potage was to be made for my lord to eate at dinner with others of his famelie, at his howfe in Lambeth marfh. But fee the wounderful chaunce, or rather the great provifion of almightie god, when his fervant came to call him to his dynner it happened that the faid reuerend father, by ouerlonge fittinge and reading in his ftudie that forenoone, more then his accuftomed howre, to have no great ftomacke to his dinner; And therfore anfwered that he would fpare his dinner for that time till night, the lyke wherof it could not be remembred [2] that he had at any time done before, willinge, neuertheles, that the howfhould fervantes fhould be fett to dinner, who eating of the poyfoned grewell were fo pitifully infected therwith, that the moft part of them neuer recouered their health to their dying daie, and two dyed forthwith, the one a gentle-

[1] Fol. 57, back. [2] Fol. 58.

man called Maiſter Bennett Curwen, and the other an ould widow, and ſo he was deliuered of that daunger, being reſerued (as it may be thought) of god for a more pretious death. This wicked perſon that did the acte was named Richard Roſe, who was after, for the ſame offence, boyled quicke in Smithfeilde in the xxijth yere of king Henries raigne. Shortly after this daungerous eſcape, there happened alſo vnto him an other great daunger at the ſame howſe in Lambeth; for ſodainly a gunne was ſhott through the topp of his howſe, not far from his ſtudie, where he accuſtomably vſed to ſitt, which made ſuch a horrible noyſe over his head, and bruſed the tyles and rafters of the howſe ſo ſore, that both he and diuers others of his ſervantes were ſodenly amaſed therat; wherfore ſpeedie ſerch was made whence this ſhott ſhould come, and what it ment, which at laſt was found to come from the other ſide of the Thameſe out of the Erle of Wilſhirs howſe, who was father to the ladie Ann. Then he [1]perceived that great malice was ment towards him, and callinge ſpeedily certaine of his ſervantes, ſaid: "Let us truſſe vp our geere and be gone from hence, for here is no place for vs to tarrie any longer." And ſo immediately departed to Rocheſter, where he remayned not longe quyett, before he heard of new trooble. What the occaſſion of this dealinge towards him was, or whether it were by the kings conſent or no, I will not certainly affirme, but ſure it is that the kinge at that time ought him his hartie diſpleaſure, and ſpake ſuch & ſo many daungerous words of him both at his table & elſwhere, that others hearing the ſame were the more imboldened to vſe violence and iniurie towards him.

After he was departed from London & ſafely come to Rocheſter, in this great diſpleaſure and daunger, he then fell to his ould trade of preaching to his flocke & viſiting of ſicke perſons, beſides an infinite number of other deeds of mercy: and at that time alſo he beſtowed great coſt vpon the reparracion of the bridge of Rocheſter. But over and above all this, he beſtowed no ſmall labour and paine in repreſſinge of hereſies, which by this time were verie much increaſed and far ſpred in this Realme. And although by his continewall travell he brought many heretickes into the waie againe, that before were

[1] Fol. 58, back.

farr ftraid and gone from the truth; yet among other hereticks [1] his moft labour was with one John frith, a verie obftinate & ftubborne wretch, whom he could never reclaime nor bring to any conformitie, and therfore was iuftly by order of lawe condemned, and after burned in Smithfeild.

And although by meanes of this great difpleafure of the king and many of his nobillitie, he ftood in great daunger of his lyfe (as before is mentioned); yet confidering the quarrell he had taken in hand, he never feemed to be one whit difmaid therat, nether yet to be moved for any worldly trooble that could happen vnto him: wherof although I could recite you many examples, yet for this time this one may fuffife. On a night, as he lay at his Mannour howfe of Hallinge neere Rochefter, a companie of theeves brake previly in the night time into his howfe, and robbed him of all his plate; which being in the morning perceived and knowne to his officers and fervantes, they were much vexed and forie through the mifchaunce, wherfore purfuite was fpeedily made after the theeves, and fuch dilligence was vfed that, before my lord knew any thinge therof, fome part of the plate was found againe in a wood ioyninge to the howfe where the theeves had paffed, which through haft in flyinge they fcattered behind them, and durft no more returne for it. When dinner time was come my lord [2] perceived vnquietnefs and heavines' amonge his fervantes more than was wont to be, for no man durft open vnto him the caufe, thinking he would have taken it fo ill; at laft, my lord miftruftinge more and more by their countenaunces of fome great harme, he afked one of them what this matter ment; but his fervant for feare durft not open vnto him the mifchaunce. "No" (faid my lord), "I meane not to dine this daie before I know what it is." "Then" (faid he), "This night a certaine number of theeves have robbed you of your plate, which is all loft and gone, faving a litle quantitie that was recouered in a wood by following them, and that," faid he, "was brought backe againe." "Is this all?" (faid my lord); "then let vs goe to dinner and be merrie, and thanke god for that we have ftill remayninge, and looke better to yt then we did to the reft before," and fo eate his dinner verie merrily and quietly.

[1] Fol. 59. [2] Fol. 59, back.

The king remayning ftill greevoufly offended with the whole Clergie of England for the ill fucceffe of the great matter of Divorce, held his perleament at Westminfter; begining after diuers prorogacions the xvjth day of Januarie in the xxijth yere of his raigne, and the year of our lorde god 1530, at which time the Clergie of the Province of Canterburie (according to their auncient cuftome) fommoned a Convocacion at Weftminfter. In this [1] parlement diuers things were bouldly propofed and ftowtly vrged againft the Clergie; and amonge other matters it was there declared what great charges the king had wrongfully bene at (as it was tearmed) about his matter of divorce in fuite to the Court of Roome, and obtayning of fundrie Inftrumentes of forraine vniverfities, and draughtes of many learned mens opinions, amounting, as it was declared, to the fomme of one hundred thowfand pounds and more; the cheef and only caufe wherof was (as they faid) the falfhood and diffimulacion of the Cardinall, and certaine others of the cheef of the Clergie; in confideracion wherof it was there demaunded to be paid amonge them.

In this matter as there wanted no Orators of the kings faction to preferre his purpofe, fo the orators wanted no wordes to debate and fett it forward to the moft, and on the contrarie part, nothing might be heard, or fcant any man durft whifper or open his mouth. But yet amonge the Convocacion there wanted not fome that fpake ftoutly againft the kings vnreafonable demaund, Amonge which this holy man was cheef, fayinge, that yt was not there falte that the king had bene at all this charge; nether was there any iuft caufe whie he fhould have fpent any one penny about this [2] bufinefs, and therfore except fome other allegacion might be made then they yet heard of, it was flatly denyed to give him any thinge at all.

Then the kinge growinge more furious fought an other waie, and fo by proceffe bringinge the whole Clergie into the kings bench, fewed the Cardinall and them in a preminire for acknowledginge the authoritie and power Legantive of the faid Cardinall Wolfey; wherin with fmall difficulte he condemned them in fhort fpace, determininge then fully with himfelf, not only to imprifon fuch and fo many of them as him felf lyked, but alfo to enter vpon there

[1] Fol. 60.   [2] Fol. 60, back.

whole poffeffions and goodes. And here I think it not amiffe to declare vnto you what I have heard of the occafion and caufe of this condemnacion in the preminire.

This Realme of Englande hath of longe time challenged (by what meanes I knowe not) a priveledge graunted (as is faid) from the See of Rome, that no legat de latere fhould enter the Realme excepte the kinge had firft fent to Rome for him; wherfore Cardinall Wolsey, eyther ignorant, forgetfull, or els making but fmall accounte, being [1] a man wounderfull ambitious and afpiringe to honour, and in fuch favour and credit then with the kinge that he durft attempt what him lyfted, made fuch meanes to the See Apoftolick, that he obtayned power legantive from the Pope that then was, and exercifed the fame a certaine fpace without the kings confent or knowledge; But yet at laft remembringe what he had done, and wayinge the daunger that depended thervpon, whileft he more diligently marked the fequell therof, in cafe the ftate of things fubiect to the courfe of fortune fhould change as many times yt happeneth; he wrought fo with the kinge that he obtayned his warrant, confirmed vnder the great feale of England, as well for that which was paft as for the reft to come. Afterward when the king, miftruftinge the Cardinalls dealinge in his great and waightie matter of divorce, began to turne his accuftomed love into extreame hatred; for the more eafie practifinge therof he vfed the helpe of Maifter Cromwell then his fervant, and in great truft with him, to gett from the Cardinall the forefaid warrant, which, lyke an vnfaithfull and trayterous fervant, the faid Cromwell ftole from his Maifter and deliuered to the kinge, who ftraight waies vpon yt charged the Cardinall with [2] a premunire vpon a ftatute of Richard the fecond, comprifing not only the Cardinall within the compaffe of that ftatute for exercifing fuch power legantive, but alfo the reft of the Clergie of the Realme for accepting and acknowledginge the fame. But the Clergie, not willing to abyde the daunger of the kings cruell difpleafure (yf by any meanes they might avoid it) graunted vnto him 100,000li by perfwafion of the kings Counfell, and thervpon defired pardon for the reft of their goods, which at laft with much adooe was promifed vnto

[1] Fol. 61. [2] Fol. 61, back.

them all, certaine perſons excepted; but yet it was not accompliſhed ouer haſtely, for before the full performance therof, a new & ſtraunge demaund was made to the Clergie in their convocacion, ſuch a one as hath not in any Chriſten Princes daies bene heard of before; and that was that they ſhould acknowledge the kinge to be their ſupreme head. This requeſt, although it was verie monſtrous and rare, yet notwithſtand the matter was fore vrged, and the kings Orators omitted noe time nor occaſion that might helpe forward their purpoſe, ſomtime by fair wordes, and ſomtimes by hard and cruell threatnings: Amonge which Maiſter Thomas Audley was a great doer, who, after ſuch time as bleſſed Sir Thomas More gave over the office of Lord chancellor, ſucceeded him in that place.

[1] When this matter was come to ſcanning in the Convocacion howſe, great hould and ſtirr was made about it; for amonge them there wanted not ſome that ſtood readie to ſet forward the kings purpoſe, and for feare of them many others durſt not ſpeake their mindes freely. But when this holy father ſawe what was towardes, and how readie ſome of their owne companie were to helpe forward the kings purpoſe, he opened before the biſhops ſuch and ſo many inconveniences by grauntinge to this demaund, that in Concluſion all was reiected and the kings intent cleane ouerthrowne for that time.

Then the kinge hearing what was done, and perceiving that the whole convocacion reſted vpon this worthie biſhop, he wrought by ſundrie meanes to bringe the matter about; and yet doubting that with overmuch haſt and vigor at the begininge he might eaſily at the firſt ouerthrowe all his intent, he ſent his Orators at another time to the Convocacion howſe, who in their owne names moved the Clergie to haue good conſideracion of this gentle and reaſonable demaund; putting them in mind what daunger and perill they ſtood in at this preſent againſt his maieſtie for their late contempt in acceptinge the Legantive power of the Cardinall, wherby they had alſo deeply incurred the daunger of the lawe, that their lande and goods were wholely at his highnes will and pleaſure, which, notwithſtanding, he hath hitherto [2] forborne to execute vpon hope of their good wills and conformities to be ſhewed to him againe in this matter.

[1] Fol. 62.   [2] Fol. 62, back.

Then the king sent for diuers of the bishopps, and certaine others of the cheef Convocacion to come to him, at his pallace of Westminster, to whom he proponed with gentle wordes his request and demaund, promising them in the word of a kinge, that yf they woulde amonge them acknowledge and confesse him for supreme head of the Church of England, he would never by vertue of that graunt assume vnto himself any more power, iurisdiccion, or authoritie over them then all other the kings of the Realme of his predicessors had done before, nether would take vpon him to make or promulge any spirituall lawe, or exercise any spirituall iurisdiccion, nor yet by any kind of meanes intermeddle himself amonge them in altering, changinge, ordering, or judginge of any spirituall busines. "Therfore, having made you" (said he) "this franke promise, I doe expect that you should deale as frankly with me againe, wherby agreement may the better continew between vs." And so the Bishops departed with heavie harts to talke further of this matter in [1] the Convocacion amonge themselves. But still it stucke sore amonge them vpon certaine inconveniences before shewed by my lord of Rochester who neuer spared to open and declare his mind freely in defence of the Church, which many others durst not so frankly doe for feare of the kings displeasure, although they were for the most part men of deep wisdome and profound learninge.

Then came the kings Counsellors againe from the kinge to knowe howe the matter spedd, seeming as though they had not knowne what was said before in the Convocacion howse before their comminge. So hotely they followed this matter, once begun for many causes, the king having in deed a further secreat meaninge then was commonly knowne to many, which in fewe yeres brake out, to the confusion of the whole clergie and temperaltie both. These counsellors there repeated vnto the Convocacion the kings wordes, which he himself had spoken to some of them, saying further, that if any man would stick now against his maiestie in this pointe it must needes declare a great mistruftfulnes they had in his highnes wordes, seeing he had made so solemne and high an oath. With this subtill and false perswasion [2] the Clergie began somwhat to thinke, and for

[1] Fol. 63.   [2] Fol. 63, back.

the moſt part to yelde to the kings requeſt, favinge this holy biſhop, who vtterly refuſed to condiſcend thervnto, and therfore erneſtly required the lordes, and others of the Convocacion to confider and take good heed what miſcheifs and inconveniences would enſewe to the whole church of Chriſt, by this vnreaſonable and vnſeemly graunt made to a temperall prince, which neuer yet to this daie was once ſo much as once demaunded before, neither can yt by any meanes or reaſon, be in the power or rule of any temporall potentate. "And therfore" (ſaid he) "yf ye graunt to the kings vaine requeſt in this matter, it ſeemeth to me to pretend an immenent and preſent daunger at hand: for what yf he ſhould ſhortly after chaunge his mind and exerciſe in deed the Supremacie over the church of this realme? or what yf he ſhould die, and then his ſucceſſor challenge the continewance of the ſame? or what yf the crowne of this realme ſhould in time fall to an infant or a woman that ſhall ſtill continewe and take the ſame name vpon them? What ſhall we then doe? whom ſhall we ſerve vnto? or where ſhall we have remedie?" The kings Counfellors to that replyed & ſaid, that the kinge had no ſuch meaninge as he doubted, [1] and then alleadged againe his royall proteſtacion & oath made in the word of a kinge. "And further" (ſaid they) "though the Supremacie were graunted to his Maieſtie ſimply & abſolutely accordinge to his demaund, yet it muſt needes be vnderſtoode and taken, that he can have no further power or authoritie by it then quantum per legem dei licet, and then yf a temporall Prince can have no ſuch authoritie and powre by gods law (as his Lordſhip (?) had there declared), what needeth the forecaſting of all theſe doubtes?" Then at laſt the Counſellors fell into diſputacion amonge the Biſhopps, of a temporall princes authoritie ouer the Clergie, but therto my lord of Rocheſter anſwered them ſo fullie, that they had no liſte to deale that waie any further, for they were in deed but ſimple ſmatterers in Divinitie to ſpeake before ſuch a Divine as he was. And ſo they departed in great anger, ſhowing themſelves openly in their owne lykenes, and ſaying that whoſoeuer would refuſe to condiſcend to the kings demand herin, was not worthie to be accounted a true and lovinge ſubiect.

[1] Fol. 64.

The Lords and other of the Convocacion feeing this kind of threatninge perfwafion, befides many other falfe practifes, and fearinge the report of the Counfellors to be made to the Kinge (whom they knew & perceaved to be all cruelly bent againft the Clergie) grew at [1] laft to a conclufion, and fo after fundrie daies argument in great ftrivinge and contention agreed in manner fully and wholly amonge them to condifcend to the kinges demaund. That he fhould be fupreame head of the church of England, and to credit his princly word fo faithfully, and folemnly promifed vnto them.

My lord of Rochefter perceiving this foden & haftie graunt only made for feare, and not vpon any iuft ground, ftood vp againe all angrie, and rebuked them for their pufillanimity in beinge fo lightly chaunged and eafilly perfwaded. And beinge verie loath that any fuch graunt fhould paffe from the Clergie thus abfolutely, and yet by no meanes able to ftaie it for the feare that was amonge them, He then advifed the Convocacion, that feeinge the kinge, both by his owne mowth, and alfo by the fundrie fpeeches of his Orators, had faithfully promifed, and folemnly fworne in the high worde of a kinge; That his meaninge was to require no further then quantum per legem dei licet, and that by vertue therof his purpofe was not to intermeddle with any fpirituall lawes, fpirituall iurifdiccion or government, more then all other his predifeffors had alwaies done before[']: yf it fo be that you are fully determined to graunt him his demaund (which I rather wifh you to denie then graunt) yet for a more trewe and plaine expofition [2] of your meaninge [3] towardes the kinge and all his pofterritie, let thefe condicionall wordes be expreffed in your graunt, quantum per legem dei licet, which is no otherwife (as the kinge and his counfellors fay) then themfelves meane. But then the Counfellors (who by that time were returned to the Convocacion howfe for fpeed of their bufines) hearing of my lord of Rochefters words, cryed vpon them with open and continuall clamour to have the grant paffe abfolutely, and to credit the kings honor in givinge them fo folemne a proteftacion and oathe. But after this time nothinge could prevaile: for then the Clergie anfwered with their full

[1] Fol. 64, back.   [2] *Expression* written under exposition.
[3] Fol. 65.

refolucion, that they nether could nor would graunt this title and dignitie of Supremacie without thefe conditionall wordes, quantum per legem dei licet. And fo the Orators departed, makinge to the kinge relation of all that was done, who, feeinge no other remedie, was of neceffitie driven to accept it in this conditionall fort, and then graunted to the Clergie pardon for their bodies and goods, fo that they fhould paie him an hundred thoufand pounds, which was paid to the laft penny.

But this refted not longe after this forte, for the Kinge within few yeres after tooke vpon him and exercifed the Supremacie of the Church of England contrarie to his promiffe, as this holy man doubted and forefawe. And in a Parliament holden at Weftminfter the xxvj[th] yere of his raigne (when the good father was in prifon [1] within the towre of London), he made an Act of Parliament by authoritie of his laye people, wherin he was confirmed Supreame head of the Church of England, without any further exception or Condition at all, framing nevertheles the wordes of that Act in fuch fort, as though the Clergie in their Convocacion had abfolutely recognized him for fupreame head before, and after caufed the fame to be annexed to his ftile as a tytle of his dignitie royall, appointinge to all fuch as fhould by any meanes withftand or gainfaie the fame, noe leffe punifhment then is dew in Cafes of high treafon, were they fpirituall or temporall, which his fucceffors hath fince that time practifed as by experience we maie fee: And yet to that acte and many other licentious and fcifmatticall doinges of the kinge, all the Bifhopps afterward agreed, only this holy bifhopp excepted.

About this time (which was in the xxiiij[th] yere of the kings raigne) this good father happened to fall into great troobte, which the king fought him by fundrie meanes. The manner of which trooble was thus. When by publicke fame the kinges intent was knowne abroade that he ment to feperat from him [2] the good queene Catherine, his moft lawfull wife, and many an other, the Realme began as it were to devide, and much talke was vfed herin, fome in favour of the kinge, and fome of the queen. But the farr greater number afwell of the learned fort as of the vulgar people ftucke

[1] Fol. 65, back.   [2] Fol. 66.

FISHER.   F

rather to the queenes part then to the kings. At the fame time one Elizabeth Barton, a yonge maiden borne in Kent, at a place called Court at Street, declared vnto fundrie perfons that many times fhe had certaine vifions revealed vnto her towchinge the kings doings in his matter of Divorce : by what meanes fhe could not tell, but (as fhe thought) they came from god. Wherin for mine owne part I will not for certaine affirme anythinge, ether with her or against her, becaufe I have heard her diuerfly reported of, and that of perfons of right good fame & eftimacion. But true it is that divers times being in her traunce (wherin fhe happened to fall verie often), fhe vttered fuch wordes towchinge the reproovinge of herefies which then began faft to fpreade, declaring what mifcheef and calamitie would infewe to this realme, by admittinge the fame, that it was thought woundurfull to be heard at the mouth of a fimple woman. She would faie that it was fhewed vnto her in her vifion, that the king had an ill intent & purpofe in him, and fpecially in that he minded to feparate himfelf and the good queen Catherin his wife a funder, and minded for his voluptuous and carnall [1] appetite to marrie an other, which by no meanes he could doe without the great difpleafure of Almightie God, for it was directly againft his holy lawes. And this matter fhe opened on a time to Maifter Richard Maifter, Parfon of Aldington in Kent, and then her ghoftlye father, faying vnto him further, that by her revelation fhe perceaved that yf the kinge defifted not from his purpofe in this great cafe of Divorce, but would needes profecute the fame and marry againe, *that* then after fuch marriage he fhould not longe be kinge of this Realme, and in reputacion of god, he fhould not be kinge therof one daie nor one howre after, and that he fhould die a fhamefull and miferable death. Likewife fhe faid and affirmed that the good vertuous queen Catherin was the kings lawfull wife, and that he could not lawfully marrie any other; but whether he did marrye any or not, yet fhould the ladie Marie, the daughter of the faid good queen, profper and raigne in the Realme, and have many frendes to eftablifh and maintaine her.

Thefe and diuers fuch lyke matters beinge opened to the faid Parfon of Aldington, he gave her advife to goe to Canterburie, and

[1] Fol. 66, back.

there to talke with M*aifter* Edward Borkinge, doctor of Divinitie, and a Mounke of Chriftes church, becaufe he was of all [1] men reputed for a learned and vertuous man; from him fhe went to M*aifter* John Deringe, an other mounke of *th*e fame houfe. Thefe good fathers, beinge marveloufly aftonied at her ftrange fpeeches, opened the fame to the moft reue*r*end father in god, William Warham, Archbifhopp of Canterbury, who i*m*mediatly after the begininge of this bufines departed this lyfe. At length her name fpredd fo wide, that fhe was much reforted vnto of manie people, and for her ve*r*tuous and avftere life was commonly called the holy maid of Kente. And fhortly after, by the advife of the reue*rend* Doctor Borkinge, fhe was profeffed a Nunn in the Priorie of S*ain*t Sepulcher, in Canterburie, where fhe continewed duringe the time of her life in great pennance and punifhment of her felf. And beinge there a Nunn profeffed, fhe after declared much of this matter to one M*aifter* Henrie Gould, a.learned man and batchelor in divinitye, and to father Hugh Rich, Warden of the Fryers obfervant*es* in Canterburie, and Richard Rifbe an other of the brothers of the fame howfe: All which before mentioned perfons greatly fett forth the name of the faid Elizabeth in their fermons and preachings to the people, fo that fhe became famous almoft throughout all the Realme. Then afterwards the forefaid Nun*n*, as well as fome other of the religious men before named, came to this moft reue*r*rend bifhopp of Rochefter, and Doctor John Adefon his Chaplin, [2] and lykewife to doctor Thomas Abell, fomtimes the queenes Chaplin, makinge them privie to the wounderfull and ftrange revelacions and fpeeches of this Nunn; from thence fhe went (by the counfell of Doctor Borking and the parfon of Adlington) to the Charterhowfe of London and Sheene, to the Nunnerye of Sion, and to the freere howfes of Ritchmount, Canterburie, and Greenwitch, declaring to them in lyke fort as fhe had done before to others, & laftly to the kinge himfelfe, then lying at Hanworth, before whom kneelinge, fhe opened all her minde as freely as fhe was able to vtter it, defiring him therfore in gods name, afwell for *th*e safetie of his owne foul, as for p*r*efervac*i*on of this moft noble realme, to take good heed what he did, and to proceed no further in this bufines. The

[1] Fol. 67. [2] Fol. 67, back.

kinge all the while gave her quyett hearinge, feeminge to all men that
were there prefent, not only content with the wordes, but alfo much
difmayde to heare them at the mowth of fo fimple a woman, and fo
difmiffed her peaceablie for *that* time to her howfe at Canterburie,
where fhe remained not longe quiet after. for now the kinge, perceivinge *that* his doings were openly knowne to the worlde, and
finding withall that the greateft part of his Realme lyked not therof
(within fhort time was lyke by fuch means as this to bringe fome
inconvenience and daunger towar*des* him yf the fame were not prevented in convenient time) [1] he fell therfore in confultac*io*n with
his flatteringe Counfell what were beft to doe in this matter, whom
he founde devided amonge themfelves, fome thinkinge good that it
fhould be handled with clemencie and pittie, and fome, on the contrarie part, with all rigor and crueltie, for an example to others. But
in the end it was refolved that pittie fhould be fett a fide, and
feveritie take place, and fo all was turned to this: That it was but
only a trayterous confpiracie between *th*e Nunn and all the fore-
named fathers and other pe*r*fons to bringe the kinge and his government into a miflykinge and hatred of the people of his realme, and to
raife a grudge between him & them, wherby they might the better be
incorraged to make a tumult and co*m*motion againft him. Wherfore
the kinge, havinge now gotten (as he thought) a good and fufficient
matter of treafon againft this good Bifhop (whom he fpecially fought
and fhott at before all others), becaufe he was privie to the caufe
amonge them; he fent for his Iudges, and certaine other lawiers, and
before them caufed the Cafe to be proponed, defiringe of them to
knowe the lawe in that pointe, and how they might all be brought
in the Cafe of high treafon. The lawiers, fitting long in confultac*io*n
of this matter, and yet knowing in manne*r* the kings minde aforehand, fell at laft to a refolution, and concluded: That the faid
Elizabeth Barton *th*e Nunn, Edward Borkinge and John Deringe,
monk*es*; Richarde [2] maifter and Henrie Golde, preift*es*, Hugh Riche
and Richard Rifbe, freers minors, were all by *th*e law in Cafe of high
treafon. But my lord of Rochefter, with Doctor Adefon his Chaplen,
and Doctor Abell, with certaine other perfons, becaufe they were not

[1] Fol. 68.   [2] Fol. 68, back.

the firſt contryvers of the matter, but only heard it reported by them, and concealed it, were by the ſaid Iudges deemed to be in the Caſe of miſpriſon of treaſon : which is the loſſe of their goods, and impriſonment of their bodies duringe the kings pleaſure.

The Kinge not havinge herin his intended deſire, becauſe he rather ſhott at the life of this good man then his goods, was faine yet to content himſelfe therwith for that time, and ſo ſhortly after the poore Nunne, with all other the religious perſons and preiſtes before mentioned, were attached and brought vp to Lambeth before the newe biſhop of Canterburie, doctor Cranmer, where by him and certaine other Commiſſioners appointed for that purpoſe, they were verie ſtrictly examined and charged with all the terror that might be, How they moſt traiterouſly, with falſe fained hipocriſie and diſſembled ſanctity, had conſpired againſt the kinge in movinge & exciting diſpleaſure and grudge between him and his people, to the intent to raiſe a Commotion in this Realme, to the [1]great daunger of his perſon, and ſubuerſion of the whole realme, and ſo finally were all ſent to the Towre of London, where they lay longe after in much miſerie, till ſuch time as by ſharpe and cruell death they ended their daies, for in a Parleament holden at Weſtminſter the xxvth yere of the kings raigne, begininge (after diuers prorogacions) the xvth day of Januarie, they were all attainted of high treaſon, and in Aprill next followinge, the ſillie Nunn was hanged and headed at Tyborne, and the reſt were alſo the ſame daie hanged, and after quartered alive. And for aſmuch as my lord of Rocheſter, Doctor John Adeſon, his Chaplen, Doctor Thomas Abell, Thomas Lawrence, Regiſter to the Archdeacon of Canterburie, & Edward Thwaytes, gentleman, did not only know of the foreſaid offence, but alſo gave credence to the offendors, wherby the ſaid offendors tooke corrage in their doinges, were all convicted of miſpriſon of treaſon, to ſuffer impriſonment during the kings pleaſure, and to forfeit vnto him all their goods, chattells, and debts. But yet for all this tirrible ſentence geven vpon this good biſhopp, nether was he impriſoned ne yet diſpoyled of his goodes for that time, although (as I heard after) he was faine to redeeme himſelf with payment of three hundred

[1] Fol. 69.

poundes for a fine, which was one whole yeres revennewe of the bifhoprick, for the king (as before is faid) ment not to fpoile his goods, which he knew to be but of fmall valew, but rather thirfted after his life, knowinge him to be (as he was indeed) a greate ftop & hinderer of all his licentious proceedings, for *that* he bare fo great a fway in *th*e convoca*cio*n howfe as he did.

[1] You have heard before how Cardinall Campegius departed out of this realme to the Popes Holyneffe, after fuch time as the queene had made her appeale to the Sea Apoftolicke, who, beinge long before this time arived at Rome, made there to the Popes Holyneffe a declaration of all his proceedings. Shortly after whofe departure, the kinge fent to the Pope Doctor Bonner and Doctor Keane, both Doctors of the Civill lawe and profound men, to treat with him of this matter as of them felves and not fent from him, who, according to their fecret commiffion geven them, dealt verie largely in the kings behalf, fignifyinge vnto *th*e Pope that all the Bifhopps and Clergie of England were fully agreed, and thought the maryage between the kinge and the queen to be vnlawfull from the begininge, and that it was therfore verie neceffarie to make a feparation between them by a fentence definitive from his Holines. The Pope, perceivinge neuertheles that they came without authoritie or Commiffion, demaunded of them a certificat vnder the Bifhops hande, and feales of this they had faid. Then the kinge labored erneftly for this certificat, which by one meanes or other was at laft gotten out vnder all their handes and feales, favinge my lord of Rochefter, who by no meanes would euer agree to yt. At length the Certificat was fent to thefe counterfett Ambaffadors, who prefented the fame [2] to the Pope. But when he perceaved this good bifhops hand and feale wantinge amonge the reft, and vnderftood alfo that it was gotten of the other bifhops rather by flaightie devifes and Compulfion then by any direct or orderlie meanes, the Inftrument was clean reiected, and reputed to noe purpofe.

Then the Pope (becaufe he confidered the cafe to be great and waightie) would in no wife proceed any further without great and fubftantiall advife, and for that purpofe called vnto him the moft

[1] Fol. 69, back.   [2] Fol. 70.

worthie Divines and Canonistes that could be gotten. Then he consulted with all the vniuersities, that at that time were ether famous or willing to be talked with. Lykewise he procured the senfures of manie famous men, set forth in their seuerall writings, amonge which one was the booke of this most worthie and learned Bishopp of Rochester, wherof some mention is before made: which booke, by the opinion and iudgment of that reuerend and famous Clerke, Alphonsus de Castro, a spanish freer of the order of minors, is (as himself writeth) of all other the most excellent and learned worke. The Pope (I saie), after so longe and dilligent examinacion in this great matrimoniall cause, settinge in his Tribunall seat & open Consistorie, with the assent and counsell of his most reuerend bretheren, the Cardinalls of the holy Church of Rome, pronounced a [1]sentence definitive, approvinge therin the foresaid matrimonie to be good and lawfull. And becaufe this sentence is perhaps vnknowne vnto many, and specially of the countrey of England, that other have not heard, or rather will not willingly heare therof, I have thought good to insert the same in this our Hystorie word for word as it was pronounced. Let vs then heare what the Pope himself saith.

Clemens papa septimus.

Christi nomine invocato in throno iusticiæ pro tribunali sedentes et solūm deum præ oculis habentes per hanc nostram definitivam sententiam, quam de venerabilium fratrum nostrorum Sanctā Romanæ Ecclefiæ Cardinalium consistorialiter coram nobis congregatorum consilio et assensu firmius in his scriptis pronuntiamus decernimus et declaramus, in causa et causis ad nos et sedem apostolicam per appellacionem per charissimam in Christo filiam Catherinam Angliæ reginam illustrem a nostris et sedis apostolicæ legatis in regno Angliæ deputatis interpositam legitime deuolutis et aduocatis, inter prædictam Catherinam Reginam, et charissimum in Christo filium Henricum octavum Angliæ regem illustrem, super validitate et invaliditate matrimonij inter eosdem reges contracti et consummati, rebusque alijs in actis causæ et causarum hujusmodi latius deductis et dilecto filio Paulo Capisucho causarum sacri Pallatij tunc Decano, et [2]propter ipsius Pauli

[1] Fol. 70, back.   [2] Fol. 71.

abfentiam, venerabili fratri noftro Jacobo Simonetæ Epi*f*copo Pifaurienfi vnius ex d*i*cti pallatij auditoribus locum tenenti, audiendis, inftruendis, et in Confiftorio no*f*tro referendis commiffis, et per eos nobis et eifdem Cardinalibus relatis et mature difcuffis, coram nobis pendentibus matrimoni*um* inter prædictos Catherinam et Henricum Angliæ reges contractum, et inde fequuta quæcunq*ue* fuiffe validum et canonicum, validaq*ue* et canonica, fuofq*ue* debitos debuiffe et debere fortiri effectus : Prolemq*ue* exinde fufceptam vel fufcipiendam fuiffe et fore legitimam. Et prefatum Henricum Angliæ regem, teneri et obligatum fuiffe et fore ad cohabitandum cum dicta Catherina Regina eius legitima coniuge, illamq*ue* maritali affectione et regis honore tractandum. Et eundem Henricum Angliæ regem ad premiffa omnia et fingula cum effectu adimplendum, condemnandum om*n*ibufq*ue* iuris remedijs cogendum et compellendum fore ; Provt condemnamus cogimus et compellimus : moleftationefq*ue* et denegationes per eundem Henricum Regem eidem Catherinæ Reginæ fuper invaliditate et fædere d*i*c*t*i matrimonij quomodo libet factas, fuiffe et effe illicitas et iniuftas. Et eidem Henrico regi fuper illas et validitatem matrimonij huj*uf*moc*l*i perpetuum filentium imponendum fore, et imponimus Eundemq*ue* Henricum Angliæ regem in expenfis in huj*uf*moc*l*i caufa & parte d*ic*tæ Catherinæ Reginæ coram nobis et dict*is* om*n*ibus legitime factis condemnandum fore, et condemnamus. Qua*rum* expenfa*rum* taxationem nobis in pofterum refervamus. Ita pronuntiamus.

Lata fuit Romæ in Pallatio apo*ft*olico publice in Confiftorio die 23 Martij a*n*no 1534.

[1] *Pope Clement the vij*^{t} .

We invocatinge the name of Chrift and fittinge iuditioufly in throwne of iuftice, havinge only before our eyes the glorie of Almightie God, by this our definitive fentence, which by the Counfell and affent of our venerable Bretheren the Cardinalls of the holy Church of Rome affembled before vs in Confiftorie. We do in thefe wrytings geve, pronounce, decree, and declare in the caufe and caufes lawfully devolved and advocated to vs and the Sea apoftolicke, by appellac*io*n brought before vs by our welbeloved daughter in Chrift, Catherin queene of England, from the Iudgment*es* of the legates

---

[1] Fol. 71, back.

deputed and fent from vs and the forefaid Sea Apoftolicke, between the forefaid queene Catherin and our welbeloved Sonne in Chrift, Henry the viij[th], the noble king of England, vpon the validitie and invaliditie of the matrimony between them contracted and confummated, and vpon other matters more largely deduced in the actes of fuch lyke caufe and caufes, and committed to our fonne Paulus Capifuchus, then deane of the Caufes of our holy pallace, and in his abfence to our reuerend brother James Simoneta, Bifhopp of Pifawria, fupplyinge the place of one of the Auditors of our faid Pallace, to be heard inftructed, and in our Confiftorie to be reported and maturely difcuffed, during the time of the matter [1]dependinge before vs; that the matrimonie contracted betweene the faid queen Catherin and kinge Henrie of England, with all other confequentes of the fame, was and is of good force and canonicall; and that they may and ought to enioy to them their dewe effects, and that the yffue betweene them heretofore borne or hereafter to be borne was & fhall be legitimate: And that the forefaid king Henrie hath, is, and fhall be bound and obliged to cohabit & dwell with the faid queene Catherin, his lawfull wife, and to intreat her with hufbandly affection and kingly honor. And that the faid kinge Henrie is condemned, and by all remedies of lawe is to be reftrayned and compelled, as we do condemne, conftraine, and compell him to accomplifh & fulfill all and finguler the premiffes effectually: And that the moleftation and refufalls by the forefaid king Henry by any manner waies made to the faid queene Catherin towchinge the invaliditie of the faid matrimonie, are prefently & alwaies from the beginninge were vnlawfull and vniuft: And that perpetuall filence concerninge all the fore faid matters and the invaliditie of the faid matrimony fhall be enioyned vnto the faid Henrie. And we do enioyne yt. And that the faid kinge Henrie of England is to be condemned, and we do condemne him in the expenfes lawfully made before vs and our faid bretheren in fuch cafe on the behalf of the faid queen Catherin: The taxation of which expenfes we referve to our felf till an other time.

So we have pronounced.

      This was publifhed in the pallace at Rome in the open Confifterie 23 martij Anno Domini 1534.

[1] Fol. 72.

[1] And thus after many trooblefome daies of fuite with great expenfes of money, ftrange devifes, and wonderfull practifes, ended this matrimoniall Cafe by this notable fentence pronounced and publifhed by *th*e head Iudge vpon earth, to whom Chrift gave the full power and authoritie of himfelf to binde and to loofe; with w*h*ich fentence and full determinac*io*n it is to be wifhed that *th*e Kinge would have fubmitted himfelf to this greate authoritie: which yf he had done no doubt but then had this noble Realme ftill continewed in that auncient florifhinge ftate of vertue, devotion, and welth wherin he found yt. Then had he p*r*eferved his owne honor and good fame, which he afterward moft worthily loft. Then had he not opened fuch a gapp to fcifmes and herefies as he did, to our vndoinge, and the manifeft perdition of his owne foul. Then had the whole ftate of *Chrift*endome ftand in much better fuertie then of longe time it hath and now of lykelyhood it doth. Then had he ftill abidden with this moft noble ladie, his lawfull wife. And then confequently had he not proceeded to this horrible fecond maryage as he did, contrarie to the found advife of this our bleffed father and of diu*er*s others, wherof enfewed afwell the death of this holy byfhop, as of many other devout and reu*er*end Abbotte*s* and Pryors, [2] religious men and priefts, befides a number of worthie perfons of the temporalitie; the lyke wherof it is to be thought, this Realme neu*er* had at one inftant before his daies. But (alas) how farr was the kinge now chaunged from the man he was, then when by advife and helpe of this holy father he wrote his moft learned booke of the Affertion of the feaven Sacramente*s* againft Luther, and what an alteration of obedience to the Sea Apoftolicke was this in him, from *th*at time in which he dedicated his faid booke to the Popes Holineffe, w*i*th thefe wordes: "Itaq*ue* etiam hac fiducia rem tentavimus et qua in ea meditati fum*us* Sanctitati tua dedicauimus vt fub tuo no*m*i*n*e (qui *Ch*r*i*ſti vicem in terris geris) publicu*m* iudiciu*m* fubeant:" And fo with this Confidence we have attempted this matter, and have dedicate to yo*ur* Holyneffe all our labour therin, to *th*e intent *th*at vnder yo*ur* name (who vpon earth doth fupplie the place of *Ch*rift) the fame may come to the publique iudgment of *th*e worlde. Many other fuch lyke places are

[1] Fol. 72, back.   [2] Fol. 73.

to be found in *that* worthie booke, who foeue*r* fhall well pervfe and read the fame.

But let vs further confider w*h*at moved this bleffed man to ftand in defence of this quarrell, and we fhall foone perceive that he had great caufe to do as he did, for although he thought in his Confcience, and by his profound learninge moft affuredly knewe, that the kinge for noe [1]caufe yet alleadged, could by the law of god make any fep*a*rac*i*on between him and his wife, this noble Princeffe, yet had he a more fecrett intelligence of the kings doings, & further intent therin then at *that* time was knowne to many others; I meane of his proceedinge to a fecond marriage with *the* lady Ann Bullen, wherof although (for the great reue*r*ence he bore to the kings perfon) he fpared to fpeake openly that which he knew for trew, yet to fome of his fecret frendes (when it might ferve to the purpofe) he would not fticke to vtter, that the kinge could not by anie meanes proceed to fuch marryage without the ruine of his honor and good name, and the ineftimable loffe of his foul for eue*r*. No, although the Pope fhoulde pronounce the firft maryage to be void & adnihillat, and that for fundrie caufes; for firft it was well knowne that even about fuch time as the king began to caft his carnall love to this ladie, Ann Bullen, the lord Henrie Perfie, fonne and heire to *the* Erle of Northumberland, chanced alfo not longe before that time to fall in love with her; and therin at laft proceeded fo farre that they were affured before good witneffes in the waie of maryage, he beinge then attendant vpon Cardinall Woolfey, and fhe wayting in the Court vpon this good queene Catherin (nether of them yet knowing *the* kings intent); [2]but when knowledge therof came to the kings eares he waxed angrie, and was much moved againft *the* lord Pearcie, infomuch as he fent in haft for the Cardinall to come to him on a time to Bridewell, and there opened vnto him all his intent and purpofe, willinge him in any wife with all the fpeed that might be, to call before him the faid lorde Percie, and to infringe his affurance by all the meanes he could devife. The Cardinall feeinge all this matter come to this effect was not a litle vnquyeted therat. Howbeit returninge home to his howfe at Weftminfter, and not for-

---

[1] Fol. 73, back.   [2] Fol. 74.

gettinge the kings Commaundement, he called the lord Percie |before him, and there in prefence of diuers of his fervantes demaunded of him with many fharpe wordes what he had done, and how farr he had proceeded in this matter. The lord Percie perceavinge this his doinge to be ill taken, and verie lykely to turne to his difpleafure, anfwerred vpon his knee with feare; That they were affured before witneffe. Then (faid the Cardinall) haft thou done lyke a lewd boye, to attempt any fuch thinge without the knowledge other of the kings Maieftie, thy father, or me, and therfore I commaund thee that thou come no more in her companie vpon paine of the kings difpleafure & mine, for by this meane thou haft gotten thee alreadie his ill will; And I will alfo fignifie vnto thy father thy bould and rafhe attempt, wherby it is lyke thou fhalt be difinherited for ever. Then the lord Perfie in moft lamentable and pittifull manner faid vnto the Cardinall (ftill kneelinge), "I moft humblie defire your graces favour herin, and that you will ftand fo much my [1]good lord as to intreate the kings Maieftie for me, for truly I have now gone fo farre in this matter, and that before many worthie witneffes that I know not how to difcharge my confcience before god, nor yet excufe my felf before men." "Whie" (faid the Cardinall) "doft thou harpe ftill vpon that ftringe? I thought thou wouldeft have fhewed thy felf penitent for thy foolifh doings, and here have promifed to relinquifh from henceforth any further attempt therin." "Truly" (faid the lord Pearcie), "fo will I with all my hart as much as in me lyeth, my confcience only referved for my former promiffe." "Well" (faid the Cardinall), "I will fignifie fo much to the kinge," and fo departed. And this was one caufe that made this reuerend man to miflyke of this fecond marriage.

An other caufe was for that there was a greate and conftant fame how the king had before carnally knowne the ladie Anns mother, which in law forbiddeth all marriage of the children for ever after, becaufe otherwife it might be dowbt that the kinge fhould marrye his owne daughter. And for fome better probabillitie therof I have heard yt reported of diuers perfons of good credit, that the Counteffe of Wilfhire her mother (as fhe happened on a time to talke with

[1] Fol. 74, back.

*th*e kinge of this matter) fodenly faid vnto him in the hearing of fundrie perfons, half in fport and halfe in earneft, thefe wordes: "Sir, for *th*e reuerence of god t⁻ke heed what you doe in marying my daughter; for yf you record yo*ur* confcience well fhe is yo*ur* owne daughter as well as mine."

[1] Lykewife it was verie evident to many *that* were about the kinge, that he co*m*monly knewe not only this ladie, Ann Bullen, before he marryed her, but alfo longe before that he knew in lyke manne*r* the ladie Marie Carie, her fifter. And thefe were caufes whie this good man thought *that* the king could not by any meanes lawfully proceed to this maryage; no, although his firft marryage had bene void and adnihillat, or though this good queen had bene dead, and the kinge free to marrie.

Other caufes there were though not of fo great importance as thefe be, yet verie iuft & probable why the kinge with his honor and fafetie of his realme could not well proceed thervnto. For firft there went a great rumour of her incontinencie and loofe lyvinge, & what inconvenienc*es* have growne in many *Chrift*ian realmes by doubtfull fucceffion of Baftardie; there needeth here noe example to be rehearfed, beinge a cafe fo well knowne to the worlde as it is; and of this it fhould feeme there was a fhrewd lykelyhood when S*ir* Thomas Wyatt (after he vnderftood of the kings intended purpofe to marrie with her) came to the kinge and declared vnto him the truth of that he knewe, doubtinge in deed *that th*e fame co*m*ming els to his knowledge by fome other meane might kindle difpleafure fecretly in his breft againft him, and fo at one time or other breake out to his confufion.

Wherfore co*m*minge (I faie) to *th*e kinge he told him plainly [2] that fhe was no fitt wife for his ma*ieft*ie, confeffinge there almoft in plaine wordes, with great feare, that himfelf had bene familier with her. Lykewife fhe was greatly fufpected, and in manne*r* notorioufly knowne of diue*rs* perfons to be an heretick, and therby verie lykely to corrupt the kinge, being fo extreamely blinded with their vnlawfull doctrine as fhe was, which after came to paffe in deed: for fhe was the firft and only perfon that of a longe time durft breake with him

[1] Fol. 75.   [2] Fol. 75, back.

in fuch matters. The effect and fruite wherof the world feeth, and this miferable countrey more and more feeleth to our vndoinge.

Now approched the time wherin this bleffed man grew to his finall and laft trooble: for at the Parlement before mentioned, wherin he was attainted of mifprifion of treafon for the matter of the nunn of Canterburie, there was alfo in the fame Parliament an other ftatute made, declaringe the eftablifhment of the kings fucceffion in the imperiall Crowne of this realme; by vertue wherof it was enacted, that the faid mariage heretofore folemnized betweene the kinge and the ladie Catherin, beinge before his older brothers wife, and by him [1] carnally knowne (as the Acte reporteth) fhould be by the authorite of that Parliament, definitively, cleerly, and abfolutely declared, deemed, and iudged to be againft the laws of Almightie god: and alfo excepted, reputed, and taken of noe valewe or effect, but vtterlie void to all intentes and purpofes, accordinge to fentence made at Donftable by Thomas Cranmer, Archbifhop of Canterburie. And that the matrimonie had and folemnifed betweene the kinge and queene Ann fhould be eftablifhed and taken for vndoubtfull, trew, fincere, and perfect, accordinge to the iudgment of the faid Archbifhopp. And that the yffue comminge of that mariage fhould be inheritable to the Crowne and gouernment of the Realme. By meane wherof the ladie Marie, being yffue of his former marriage, was difherited and difabled to all intentes and purpofes. And yf any perfon, of what eftate or condition foeuer he be, fhall by wrytinge, printing, or any exterior Acte or deed procure or doe any thinge, to the preiudice, flaunder, difturbance, or derogation of the faid matrimony, or the yffue growing of the fame, that euerie fuch perfon fhould be deemed and iudged as a high Traytor, and fhould fuffer fuch paines and loffes as in Cafe of high treafon is provided. And further, yf any perfon fhould, by word or fpeech only, without wrytinge or doinge, vtter or publifh any thinge in derogacion [2] of this matrimonie, that everie fuch offence fhould be taken and adiudged for mifprifion of high treafon, and the offenders to fuffer imprifonment during the kings pleafure, and to loofe to him all their goods, chattells, and debts. And that for offendinge in any of thefe treafons or mifprifions, no priveledge nor

[1] Fol. 76. [2] Fol. 76, back.

immunitie of Sanctuarie within this Realme fhould ferve. Certaine other things there be alfo contained within the fame Acte, as by readinge of the fame ftatute may appeare more at large. But, laftly, it is concluded that for the better and more fure keepinge & obferving of this Acte, afwell the nobles of this realme, fpirituall and temporall, as all other fubiectes of the fame, fhall make a corporall oath, That they fhall truly and conftantly obferve, defend, and keepe to the vttermoft of their cunninge, will, and powre the whole effect and contentes of this Statute. The wordes of which oath (although they be not expreffed at large in the Statute) were thefe: Ye fhall fweare to beare faith, truth, and obedience all only to the kings maieftie, and to his heires of his bodie of his moft deere and intirely beloved lawfull wife, queen Ann, begotten and to be begotten. And further, to the heires of our foueraigne lord according to the limitacion [1] in the Statute, made for fuertie of his fucceffion in the crowne of this Realme mentioned and contayned, and not to any other within this realme, noe forraine authoritie or Potentate. And in Cafe any oath be made or hath bene made by you to any perfon or perfons, that then ye to repute the fame as vaine and annihilat, and that to your cunninge, witt, and vttermoft of your power, without guile, fraud, or other vndew meanes, ye fhall obferve, keepe, maintaine, and defend the faid Acte of Succeffion, and all the whole effects and contents therof, and all other Actes and Statutes made in confirmacion and for execucion of the fame, or of any thinge therin contained: and this ye fhall doe againft all manner of perfons of what eftate, dignitie, degree, or condicion foeuer they be: and in no wife do or attempt, nor to your powre fuffer to be done or attempted directly, any thinge or thinges prively or apertly, to the lett, hinderance, daunger, or derogation therof or of any part of the fame, by any manner of meanes, or for any manner of pretence, fo helpe you God and all Sainets, And the holy Evangelifte.

This oath, although it was not in thefe wordes expreffed in the Statute (as is before faid), and therby not of any fuch force that any man was compellable by vertue of that lawe to take yt, yet it fo pleafed [2] the Kinge and his Counfellors of their owne authoritie to

[1] Fol. 77.   [2] Fol. 77, back.

have it framed, and lykewife tendred to all fuch as were called
before the Commiffioners for that caufe authorifed: and in the end
of that feffion of parliament (which was the xxxth of March) it was
offred to all the lordes of the higher howfe, both fpirituall and
temporall, and lykewife to the Commons in the lower howfe; wherof
moft of both howfes accepted it with heavie hartes (only my lord of
Rochefter except), who openly refufed to fweare it. Neuertheles he
was winked at for that time, and nothing faid to him. And fo the
Parliament beinge ended he departed home to his Pallace of Rochefter
where he had not remayned above the fpace of four daies, but a letter
came to him from the Archbifhop of Canterburie and certaine other
Commiffioners, willinge him perfonally to appeare before them at
Lambeth, in the faid Archbifhops howfe, by a certaine daie expreffed
within that letter, all excufes fett apart. This letter beinge once
knowne and heard of within his howfe, caft fuch a terror and feare
amonge his fervantes, and after amonge other his frendes in the
countrey, that nothinge was there to be heard of [1] but lamentacion
and mourninge on all fides: Howbeit the holy man, nothinge at all
difmaid therat (as a thing that he daily and howrly looked for before),
called all his familie before him, and willed them to be of good
cheere, and to take noe care for him, fayinge that he nothinge
doubted but all this fhould be to the glorie of God, and his owne
quietneffe. "And for that" (faid he), "I beinge once gone, you
may doubte of the time of my returne hither to you againe, I have
willed my Steward to confider euerie of you with a portion of my
goodes as far as they extend, defiringe god to fend both you and me
his grace;" and fo turninge his backe lefte them all weepinge, and
went about other bufinefs. And callinge his officers to him to confult
for the difpofition of his goods, he firft allotted to Michaell howfe
in Cambrige (where he was brought vp at learninge) a hundred
pounds, which was after paid to the howfe in goulde. An other
portion he caufed to be devided amonge his fervantes, alowinge euery
one of them a rate according to his place and worthines. Lykewife
to poore people in Rochefter he affigned an other fome to be dif-
tributed. The reft he referved for himfelf to defend his neceffitie in

[1] Fol. 78.

prifon, where he accounted himfelf fure as foone as he was come before the Commiffioners, alwais refervinge vnto the Colledge of Saint John in Cambrige fuch percells of goods as he before had geven them, and borrowed againe of them by his wrytinge, though in deed his good meaninge in that point was neuer fulfilled, as after fhall be declared. The next daie he fett forward his iorney towards Lambeth, and paffing through Rochefter, there were by that time affembled a great number of people of [1] that Cittie and countrey aboute to fee him departe, to whom he gave his bleffinge on all fides, as he ridde through the Cittie bare headed. There might you haue heard great waylinge and lamentinge: fome cryinge *that* they fhould neuer fee him againe. Some others faid, woe worth they that are the caufe of his troobie; others cryed out vpon the wickednes of the time to fee fuch fight; euery one vtteringe his greefe to others as their mindes ferved them. Thus paffed he till he came to a place in the waie called Shooters hill, nigh twenty miles from Rochefter, on the topp wherof he refted himfelf, and deffended from his horfe; and becaufe the howre of his refection was then come, which he obferved at dew times, he caufed to be fett before him fuch victualls as were thither broughte for him of purpofe, and there dyned openly in the ayre, his fervants ftandinge round about him, and fo came to London that night. And this precife order of dyett he vfed longe before, becaufe the Phifitians thought, and he feared him felf to be entred into a confumption. When the daie of his appearance was come, he prefented himfelf before the byfhopp of Canterburie, the lorde Awdeley, Chauncellor of England, and Maifter Thomas Cromwell, the kings fecretarie, and certaine other commiffioners authorifed vnder the great feale to tender the oath to him and others, they fittinge then at Lambeth, where he found at the fame time Sir Thomas Moore and [2] Maifter Doctor Wilfon, fomtimes the kings Confeffor, who both had refufed *th*e oath a litle before his cominge, and thervpon Sir Thomas Moore being committed to *th*e cuftodie of the Abbot of Weftminfter, Doctor Wilfon was forthwith fent to the towre of London. Againft *th*e fame daie all the Clergie of London were alfo warned to come thither about the fame purpofe, wherof fewe or none refufed the

[1] Fol. 78, back.   [2] Fol. 79.

FISHER.

oath for that time. Then was he called into the Chamber before them, and there my lord of Canterburie put him in remembrance of the late Act of Parliament, wherin is provided an oath to be miniftred to all the kinges maiefties fubiects for the fuertie of his fucceffion in the crowne of this realme, "which oath" (faid he), "all the lordes, both fpirituall and temporall, haue willingly taken, only your lordfhip except. And therfore his maieftie holdeth himfelf greatly difcontent with you, and hath by his Commiffion appointed vs to call you before vs, and to offer you the oath once againe, which we have here prefent;" and therwith laying the oath before him, demaunded of him what he faid to yt. Then faid my lord of Rochefter, "I praie you let me fee the oath, and confider a litle vpon it." Then the Commiffioners, confultinge a litle amonge them felves, graunted him fpace for foure or five daies, and fo he departed againe to his owne howfe in Lambeth Marfh where he lodged.

[1]Duringe the time of his lyinge there many of his frendes came to vifitt him, and as it were to take their leaves of him, thinkinge to fee him no more after that day: amonge which the maifters and fellowes of Saint Johns College in Cambrige, not forgettinge their great benefitt receaved at his handes, fent vp two of their companie, called Maifter Seton and Maifter Brandfbe, partly to falute and vifitt him in the name of the whole howfe, and partly to defire of him the confirmacion of their Statutes vnder his feale, which himfelf longe before had made and drawne in writing, but yet never confirmed. And therefore doubting much the time of his imprifonment to be verie neare at hand, their humble fuite was that it would pleafe him to alowe the fame ftatutes vnder his feale before he went to prifon: but to that he anfwered that he would firft reade and confider of them once more, and then (if he lyked them) he would fulfill their requeft. "Alas" (faid they), "we feare the time is now fo fhort for you to read them before you goe to prifon." "Then," faid he, "I will read them in prifon." "Naie" (faid they), "that we thinke will hardlie be brought to paffe." "Then" (faid he), "let gods will be done, for I will neuer alowe vnder my feale that thinge [2]which I haue not well and fubftantially veiwed and confidered:" wherfore

[1] Fol. 79, back.   [2] Fol. 80.

thefe two fellowes departed without their purpofe. But fhortly after, when this good father was in prifon, and things began to alter and change, the byfhop of Canterburie and M*aifte*r Cromwell, the kings Secretarie, with certaine others, by vertue of a commiffion from the kinge, made a new booke of Statute*s*, and fent them downe vnder their authoritie to the Colledge : which new ftatute*s* beinge receaved, then were the ould then made by the Bifhop of Rochefter, pronounced void and of none effect, and therfore the bookes to be laid awaie, and difpofed at their pleafure. At the fame time was Prefedent in that howfe one M*aifte*r George Cowper, a Bacheler in divinitie, and a right well learned and reue*r*end man. This M*aifte*r Cowper, havinge one of the ould Statute bookes remayninge in his cuftodie (as by vertue of his office belonged vnto him), was loath to deface or caft it awaie for his fake that made them, but ftudyinge with himfelf what were beft to be done w*i*th *the* booke, agreed at the laft to geve the fame to fome bodie to be kept for a remembrance of that holy man, and fo vpon fome fpeciall fancie (as it feemed) gave them to a yonge fellow of that howfe ftanding by called Thomas Watfon, faying to him, "hould, take this booke of my guifte, and keep it well, for the time may [1] come that thou fhalt live and reftore it to the howfe, and fo bring the ftatutes into their force againe." And in deed (as this good man faid) it came after to paffe, for that yonge man profpered in his ftudies fo fingulerly well, that he came to great honou*r*, eftimac*i*on, & credit, and beinge many yeres after elected M*aifte*r of that howfe, reftored againe thofe good Statute*s*, which ftoode in force till wickednes againe gott the vpper hande. But fince that, for his fpeciall merittes, he beinge moft worthily promoted to the Bifhoprick of Lincoln, is for his great and profound learninge accounted a rare man in his time.

The day beinge at laft come when this bleffed man fhould geue anfwere before the Com*m*iffioners, whether he would accept the Oath or not, he p*r*efented himfelf againe vnto them, fayinge, "That he had pervfed the fame oath with as good deliberac*i*on as he could, but that it being framed in fuch fort as it is, by no meanes he could accept yt with fafetie of his Confcience. Neue*r*theles" (faid he),

[1] Fol. 80, back.

"to fatiffie the kings maieſties will and pleafure, I can be content to fweare to fome part therof, fo that my felf may frame yt with other conditions, and in other fort then it now ftandeth; and fo both mine owne confcience fhall be the better fatiffyed, and his maieſties doings the better iuftified and warranted by lawe."

[1] But to that they anfwered that the kinge would by no means lyke of exceptions or Conditions; "and therfore," faid my lord of Canterburie, "you muft anfwere directlie to our queftion, whether you will fweare the oath or noe." Then faid my lord of Rochefter, "yf you will needs haue me to anfwere directly, my anfwere is, That forafmuch as mine owne confcience cannot be fatiffied, I do abfolutly refufe the oath:" vpon which anfwere he was fent ftraightway to the Towre of London, where he remained verie clofe locked and fhutt vp in a ftronge prifon, without the companie of any perfon more then one fervant to helpe him in his neceffitie, becaufe he was aged; and this was done on tuefdaie the xxj[th] of Aprill, in the yere of our lord god 1534, and the xxv[th] yeare of the Kings Raigne, being the laft daie of his raigne for that yere.

After he had lyen in prifon fix mounths and more, the Parliament began againe at Weftminfter vpon prorogacion in the xxvj[th] yere of the kings raigne, the third daie of November. This Parliament, although it were but fhort (for yt continued but five and fortie daies), yet were the matters within it both great and waightie. Amonge which one Act was made for ratifyinge the Oathe made in the laft Parliament towching the Succeffion, for the refufinge wherof this good bifhop was committed to prifon (as ye have heard before): for ye fhall [2] vnderftand, that although this oath was miniftred to diuers perfons (wherof the moft accepted it for feare), and fome refufed it that were forthwith imprifoned, yet was not the fame euer warranted by lawe, nether yet any man compellable by that law to take yt before the makinge of the fecond Acte. And therfore feeinge it fo fell out that this good father was by their owne lawes wrongfully imprifoned for refufing this oath, yt was now ordered that his wrongfull imprifonment was to be iudged and accounted rightfull from the begininge by this Acte of Parliament.

[1] Fol. 81.   [2] Fol. 81, back.

Then was there an other Statute made in the fame Parliament wherby the kings heires and Succeffors, contrarie to his former promiffe folemlie made to the Convocation in the word of a kinge, fhould be taken, accepted, and reputed (for fo be the verie termes of *the* Statute) the one fupreame head in earth of the Church of England, called Anglicana Ecclefia, to have and inioy the fame as a title & ftile to his emperiall Crowne, with all hono*ur*s, iurifdicc*io*ns, authorities, and privileges to the fame belonginge, and fhould have full power and authoritie as himfelf lifteth: to vifitt, repreffe, redreffe, reforme, order, [1]correct, reftore, and amend all herefies, abufes, erro*ur*s, and offences whatfoeue*r* they were, as fully and amply as the fame might or ought to be done, or corrected by any fpirituall authoritie or iurifdicc*i*on. And wheras the Convocac*i*on gave him this tytle in the xxij[th] yere of his raigne, with much adooe (as ye haue readd before), and yet not fimply, but with thefe conditionall words, quantu*m* per legem dei licet; now were thefe wordes forgotten, and all was taken by this Acte as of the laie people, without any condic*io*n at all; or mention of thefe wordes, even as this holy man forefawe, and had given warninge aforehand. And that it might the more eafily be wrought, the kinge kept this good Bifhop faft in prifon all the Parliament time, lefte he, being amonge the lordes in the higher howfe, might (as he had done before) hinder the matter, which doubtles to the vttermoft of his powre he would have done in deed, not only in this Acte, but alfo in fundrie other actes, both in this Parliament and in other Parliamente*s* after, wherin the Church of England was vtterlie ruined, fpoyled, and quyte overthrowne. In the fame Parlement it was further enacted, that if any manne*r* of perfon fhould, by word or deed, malicioufly pr*e*fume to denie the title of Supremacie, that then eue*r*y fuch perfon fhould be reputed and taken as an high trayto*ur*, and to fuffer and abide fuch loffes & paines [2]as in cafes of high treafon is provided. And here I cannot omitt to declare vnto you what a bufineffe was in the Parliament howfe when this Acte was made: for there were many that thought the Lawe verie hard and rigorous, to condemne a man of high treafon for fayinge the kinge is not fupreame head of the

[1] Fol. 82. [2] Fol. 82, back.

Church : for fome time a man might faie it negligently and vnawares, and fomtimes in fporte by way of talke ; and therfore except dewe proof could be made, that the wordes were fpoken malicioufly, the common howfe was verie loath to paffe the Acte at all. This was debated amongft them for many daies, fo that at laft this word (malicioufly) was expreffed in the Acte, though afterward it ferved to noe purpofe at all.

Duringe the time that this bleffed man lay thus clofely imprifoned, the kinge fent to him divers of his counfell, and fomtimes certaine of the Bifhops, and fomtimes other lay men, that were learned, to perfwade with him to take the Oath of Succeffion, but all in vaine, for fuch was his intire conftancie, that nether paine of his imprifonment—which to a weake and ould man could not be fmall—nor yet the faire flatteringe wordes, which they that were fent [1] from the kinge, with no fmall fhewe of eloquence vfed towards him, could at all move him to take fuch oath againft his confcience : no, although he might wynne therby (as him felf faid) the whole worlde. Now was it fo that even about the verie fame time, or verie foone after that he was thus committed to the Tower, the moft famous and worthie man, Sir Thomas Moore, his companion and fellowe in trooble, was alfo committed to the fame place for lyke refufall of that Oath. This worthie man, as he was for his finguler witt farr surpaffinge any that euer yet hath bene heard or read of in this Realme, and rarely elfewhere, fo for learninge it was verie hard to finde a Laie man of that time his lyke. When worde was brought to my lord of Rochefter by his man, that Sir Thomas Moore was brought thither prifoner, he began ftraight waie to conceive a certaine Ioye, being gladd, no doubt, of fo good & faithfull companye as he therby hoped, in having now fuch a worthie companion in this great and worthie caufe ; wherfore, as foone as he had opportunitie, he fent him his lovinge and hartie Commendacion, receivinge from him the lyke againe. And after that, being in time fome what releafed of that clofe and hard imprifonment that at the firft they fuffred, they would now and then falute one an other fecretly by their mutuall letters, which continewed for a time, to both their

[1] Fol. 83.

exceedinge comfortes: Till ¹at length, God takinge pittie vpon their innocent foules, in thefe longe and trooblefome afflictions of their bodies, was pleafed to accept their good harts and wills, that fo zealoufly fought and labored to be with him; for he permitted one letter at laft to be taken, which my lord of Rochefter had written to Sir Thomas Moore, and fent by his owne fervant, which letter, being brought to the Leiutenant, he forthwith fent it to the Kings Counfell, by whom it was opened and reade, contayninge his harty requeft made to Sir Thomas Moore, to know what he had faid before the Counfell at a certaine time (when he was called before them within the Towre), towchinge the divorce, and receaving the oath limited in the new acte of Parliament; and in the fame letter he alfo declared what anfwere himfelf had made before them, being hardly vrged in the fame matters a daie or two before. This letter being thus knowne to the kinge and the Counfell, was greevoufly taken by them all, conceivinge therby ftraight waie, that much conference had bene betweene them longe together. Wherfore they were more ftraightly imprifoned then euer they had bene before. Then was my lord of Rochefters man (that was meffenger betweene them) verie clofely fhutt vp alfo, and tirribly threatened to be hanged, in cafe he did not confeffe the truth in all fuch queftions as fhould be demaunded of him, amonge which one queftion was: how many ²letters he had from time to time carried betweene his maifter and Sir Thomas Moore, who, fearing much his life, and beinge but a fimple fellowe, confeffed that he had carried about fixteen or feventeen letters, but of the contentes therof he knewe nothinge, becaufe they were fealed. Howbeit, fome of them were written with inke, and fome with cole. When this matter came to the knowledge of the two prifoners, noe marvaile though they thought them felves greeved, and were verie forie for their poore man, whose Cafe they more lamented then their owne: for towching that matter they had in hand, they were both fully agreed, though thefe letters had neuer bene, as after by their doinges it appeared further to the worlde. But at their araignment thefe lettres were hainoufly laid to both their charges, and taken as a confpiracie betweene them, wherby the one

¹ Fol. 83, back.   ² Fol. 84.

comforted the other in their wilfull obftinacie, becaufe their anfwers were alwaies alyke. When after diuers meanes vfed, the kinge faw that no waie would ferve, he fent on a daie to this conftant byfhopp the lord Chauncellour Awdley, the Duke of Suffolk, the Erle of Wilfhire, Maifter Secretarie Crumwell, and certaine others of his privie Councell, to fignifie vnto him the new lawe that was lately made fince his imprifonment for the kings fupremacie, contayninge within it the paine of highe treafon to all fuch as [1] fhould directly gainfaie, or by any manner waies withftand the fame: "wherfore" (faid they) "we are now come vnto you in his maiefties name, to vnderftand whether you are content to acknowledge and confeffe the fame, as other lordes fpirituall and temporall, and the commons in the name of the whole realme have done, or noe?" This matter, as it was both great and waightie, fo it began to towch him as neere as his fhirte; for vpon anfwere of this Cafe he knewe right well his life refted, for he confidered deepely with himfelf, both by that which he had before read in the Statute, and alfo the report which he had heard of others, that yf by plaine and expreffe wordes he fhould fay the king was not fupreme head of the Church of England, then were he in daunger of his life, becaufe it was plaine treafon by the new ftatute. And knowinge againe by his learninge, that notwithftandinge this lawe, the kinge nether was, nor by any right (the law of god repugninge) could iuftly be fupreame, he was perfwaded that to confeffe that openly in his mowth which his confcience taught him to be cleane falfe and vntrewe, were nothinge els but manifeftly to incurre the difpleafure of god, and indaunger his foul: wherfore, being in great perplexitie with himfelf what anfwere he might make for the prefervacion of his life in this worlde, and his foul [2] in the other world to come; at laft, for faving of them both together, he made this wife and grave anfwere:

"My lords, you haue here demaunded of me a queftion foe dowbtfull to anfwere, that I wott not almoft what to faie to yt with mine owne fafetie, and therfor this new Acte feemeth to me much lyke a two-edged fworde; for yf I anfwere you directly, with denyall of the kings Supremacie, then am I fure of death; and yf,

[1] Fol. 84, back. [2] Fol. 85.

on the contrarie part, I acknowledge the fame contrarie to my owne confcience, then am I fure of the loffe of my foule; wherfore (as neare as I can to avoid both daungers) I fhall defire your Lordfhipps to beare with my filence, for I am not minded to make anie direct anfwer to it at all."

The lordes, and others of the kings Councell, hearinge his anfwer, were nothinge fatiffied nor contented therewith, wherfore they began to vrge him yet a litle nearer, and the lord Chauncellour (in the name of the reft) faid vnto him : That it were good he did a litle better confider of this matter; "for thefe kind of wordes" (faid he) "will by no meanes lyke the kings maieftie." And then he repeated vnto him how the kings grace was informed of the mutuall conference that had paffed betweene him and Sir Thomas Moore by fundrie letters, which he tooke in verie ill parte; "and therfore" (faid he), "yf you fhall now ftand in this manner againft him, you fhall more exafperat his greevous [1] indignation and difpleafure, and geve him good caufe to thinke that you deale more ftubbornly with him then ftandeth with the dutie of a good fubiecte."

To that my lord of Rochefter anfwered, that towching that which had paffed between him and Sir Thomas Moore, he wifhed now with all his hart that they were all there readie to be fhewed, affirminge vpon his word and promiffe, that the effect of the moft of them was no other thinge then frendlie falutacion. "And further" (faid he), "knowinge that Sir Thomas Moore was fundrie times fince his imprifonmente called before your lordfhipps and others, as I was, to anfwer to fuch queftions as there were proponed vnto him, towchinge the new ftatute, I was defirous to knowe his anfweres, becaufe of the greate opinion I haue in his profound learninge and finguler witt. And, lyke as I was defirous to know his anfwere, fo I aduertifed him of mine. And where it is thought that the kings maieftie will be much difpleafed with me with this kind of doubtfull anfwere; truly no man fhall be more forie for it then I. But where the cafe fo ftandeth, as by mine open and plaine anfwere with fatiffyinge his maiefties pleafure, I cannot efcape the difpleafure of Almightie god, I thinke it the more tollerable on my part yf I vfe filence, and do truft that his grace will fo accept it."

[1] Fol. 85, back.

[1]Then faid Mai/ter Cromwell: "wherby thinke you (more then other men have done) that in fatiffyinge the kinges Maie/tie herein, you fhould difpleafe god?" "Becaufe" (faid he) "I know how mine owne confcience ftandeth, and fo do I not an other mans." "Yf your Confcience be fo fetled" (faid my lord Chancellour), "I doubt not but you can render fome good caufe therof, and that ye can be content to open the fame to vs." "In deed." (faid he), "I thinke I am able to render you a good fufficient caufe whie my confcience fo ftandeth, and could alfo be content to declare you the fame, might I do yt with mine owne fafetie, and without offence to the kinges maie/tie and his lawes." whervnto no man anfwered any more for that time, but, callinge for the Leiuetennant, he was deliuered againe vnto him againe with a verie ftraite charge, that no further conference or meffage fhould paffe between him and Sir Thomas More, or any other. And fo they went to the kinge, & made report of all that was done: after the which time the leivetenant (accordinge to his great charge) looked more narrowly to them both then before he had donne, fo that noe knowledge paffed between them more then by gods holy fpiritt, which vndowbtedly directed them both in all their fayings and doings: for in all their examinacions after their anfweres were euer agreeable.

Thus were thofe two notable and worthy perfons from day to daie labored and wrought by the kings Councell [2]fundrie waies to confeffe and acknowledge this new Act of Succeffion, and to receive the oath for obfervinge the fame; But for all that could be done, nether of them would be euer brought fo farre, wherfore feeinge that none of thefe meanes would ferue, the Councell vfed a new craftie and fubtill devife to deceive them both (yf yt might have bene), by gevinge out falfe rumors of the one to the other; for at a folemne daie appointed, when my lord of Rochefter was called before them, and there fore vrged to take the oath, they threatned erneftly vpon him that he refted himfelf altogether vpon Sir Thomas Moore, and that by his perfwafion he ftoode fo ftiflie in the matter as he did; and therefore to drive him from that howlde, they tould him plainly, and put him out of dowbt, that Sir Thomas Moore had receaved the

[1] Fol. 86.   [2] Fol. 86, back.

oath; and fhoulde therfore finde the kinge his good lord, and be verie fhortly reftored to his full libertie with his Graces favour, which did at the firft caft this good father into fome perplexitie and forrowe for Sir Moores fake, whom for his manifould divine guiftes he tendered and highly reverenced, thinkinge it had bene trewe in deed, becaufe he miftrufted not the falfe traines of the Councellours. But yet could not all this move him to take the oath.

Lykewife when Sir Thomas Moore was [1]called before them, they would perfwade with him as they did before with my lord of Rochefter, makinge him beleeue that he would never have ftood thus longe, but for my lord of Rochefter, and then in the end tould him that he was content to accept the oath, which Sir Thomas Moore fufpected greatly to haue been trewe, and yet not altogether trewe; for that it was fo geven out by the lordes (of whofe flaights he was not ignorant), but becaufe it was a common talke amonge diuers others as he vnderftood by the report of maiftrifs Margaret Roper, his daughter, who vpon fpeciall fuite had free acceffe to her father for the moft time of his imprifonment. She had thus reported vnto him vpon occafion of talke once with my lord Chauncellour, who on a time as fhe was futor to him for her fathers increafe of libertie, anfwered her, that her father was a great deal too obftinate & felf willed, faying that there were no more in the Realme that fticked in this matter but he and a blind bifhopp (meaninge my lord of Rochefter), "who is now content" (faid he) "with much adooe to accept the oath, and fo I wifh your father to doe, for otherwife I can do him no good." And the lyke anfwere my lord Chauncellor made alfo to the ladie Ales Alington, the wife of Sir Giles Alington, and daughter of Sir Thomas Moores laft wife; when fhe at an other time before was futor for her father-in-law, Sir Thomas Moore, in the fame cafe.

[2]The kinge feeinge himfelf by all this neuer the nearer to his purpofe, began then to feeke daily new inventions, either to bringe him to confeffe his fupremacie accordinge to this new Acte, or els for denyinge the fame to intrapp him into fuch daunger as is provided in the faid Acte. Then came to him at feuerall times

[1] Fol. 87.   [2] Fol. 87, back.

byſhopp Stokeſly of London, biſhopp Stephen Gardiner of Wincheſter, biſhopp Tunſtall of Durham, with certaine other biſhops to perſwade him to yelde to the kings demand. And yet no doubt but moſt of them did this againſt their ſtomacks, and rather for feare of the kings diſpleaſure (in whom they knew there was no mercie) then for any truth they thought in the matter; for I have credibly heard ſaie that Biſhopp Stokeſly all his lyfe after, when he had occaſion to ſpeake of this buſineſſe, would ernestly weepe and ſaie: "Oh, that I had holden ſtill with my brother Fyſher and not lefte him when time was:" And for the Biſhopp of Wincheſter, my ſelf have diuers times heard him, ſomtime in the pulpitt openly, and ſomtime in talke at dinner amonge the lordes of the Councell, and ſometime in other places verie ernestly accuſe himſelf of his behaviour and [1]doings at that time: I have alſo heard the right reuerrend & learned father Doctor Thomas Harding, ſometime his Chaplen and ghoſtly father, ſaie that oftentimes in much of his feacrett talke amonge his Chaplins he would ſo bitterly accuſe himſelf of his doings, in that and ſuch like buſineſs of thoſe daies, that at laſt the teares would fall from his eyes abundantly, and finallie in the daies of kinge Edward the ſixt, being convented before the kings Commiſſioners, and there greatly vrged to proceed yet further, accordinge to the fruites of that time; he not only retracted before them all his former doings, but alſo ſuffred himſelf to be deprived of his great dignitie, and liuinge with ſharpe impriſonment within the towre of London the ſpace of five yeres and more, mindinge there to haue recouered the thinge which he before had loſt; I meane the bleſſed ſtate of martyrdome, yf god had bene ſo pleaſed; or els in place therof to continew a godlie confeſſor, remayninge a perpetuall priſoner all his daies, for a iuſt and trewe deſerved pennaunce of his offence. Howbeit it ſhortly after fell out otherwiſe, in the Raigne of this moſt noble and vertuous Queen Marie; for after god had once placed her in the gouernment and crowne of this realme, ſhe not only reſtored the auncient & Catholic religion throughout the ſame realme, but alſo deliuered him out of priſon with the biſhopp of Durham, before named, and diuers others, who laie there in lyke ſorte and almoſt the lyke ſpace that the biſhop of wincheſter did.

[1] Fol. 88.

[1]Thefe Bifhopps (I faie) perfwaded thus continewally with this holy man, fomtimes one & fomtimes an other, but all in vaine; for by no meanes would he be wonne to fwarue one Iote from that which by his learninge he knewe to be iuft and trewe.

At an other time came to him by the kings commaundment, fix or feaven bifhopps at once, to treat with him in lyke fort as the others had done feuerally before. And when they had declared their intent and caufe of their comminge, he made anfwere again in thefe, or lyke wordes,—" My Lords, it is no fmall greefe to me that occafion is geven to deale in fuch matters as thefe be, but it greeveth me much more to fee and heare fuch men as you be perfwade with me therin feeinge it concerneth you in your feueral[2] charge, as deeply as it doth me in mine, and therfore me thinketh it had bene rather our partes to fticke together in repreffinge thefe violent and vnlawfull intrufions and iniuries dayly offred to our common mother, the holy Church of Chrift, then by any manner of perfwafions to helpe or fett forward the fame. And we ought rather to feeke by all meanes the temporall diftruccion of the fo [3]ravenous woolves, that daily goe about wyrryinge and devowringe euerlaftinglie, the flocke that Chrift committed to our Charge, and the flocke that himfelf dyed for, then to fuffer them thus to range abroad. But (alas) feeing we do it not, ye fee in what perrill the Chriften State nowe ftandeth: We are befeeged on all fides, and can hardly efcape the daunger of our enemie: And feeinge that iudgment is begone at the howfe of god, what hope is there lefte (if we fall) that the reft fhall ftande! The fort is betrayed even of them that fhould have defended it. And therfore feeinge the matter is thus begunne, and fo faintly refifted on our parts, I feare we be not the men that fhall fee the ende of the miferie. wherfore feeing I am an ould man and looke not longe to live, I minde not by the helpe of god to trooble my confcience in pleafing the king this waie whatfoeuer become of me, but rather here to fpend out the remnant of my old daies in prayinge to god for him." And fo their communicacion beinge ended, the byfhops departed, fome of them with heavie harts, and after that daie came no more to

[1] Fol. 88, back.
[2] " feueral" underlined and "in your feueral" written in margin.
[3] Fol. 89.

him. But within a litle space after these bishops were thus gone, his owne man *that* kept him in the prison beinge but a simple fellowe, and hearing all this talk, fell in hand with him about this matter and said: "Alas (my Lorde), [1] why should you sticke with the kinge more then the rest of the byshops haue done, who be right well learned and godly men, doubt you not he requireth noe more of you, but only to saie he is head of the Church, and me thinketh *that* is no great matter, for your lordshipps may still thinke as you list." The byshopp perceivinge his simplicitie and knowinge he spake of good will and love towards him, said vnto him againe in the waie of talke: "Tush, tush, thou art but a foole, and knowest litle what this matter meaneth, but hereafter thou maist knowe more. But I tell thee it is not for the Supremacie only that I am thus tossed and troobled, but also for an oath" (meaninge the oath of the king's succession) "which yf I would have sworne, I doubt whether I should euer haue bene questioned for the Supremacie or noe; but god being my good lord I will never agree to any of them both. And this thou maist saie another daie thou heardest me speake when I am dead and gone out of this worlde."

The Kinge beinge still desirous to take all the vantage againft this good father, that might be found by vertue of his new lawe, and yet by all that he had hitherto spoken or done, not able to take ynough [2] for his purpose, began now a new waie how to intrap him by pollicie, which although it were verie vncharitable, and not standinge with a Princes Maiestie, yet such was the king's malice againft this holy man, that so he might compasse his purpose, he respected nether right nor wronge, truth nor falshood, honor nor shame. The manner of this new invented pollicie was this. About the begininge of Maie after this blessed father had bene prisoner somwhat more then a yeare the kinge sent vnto him one Maister Richard Rich, being then his generall Solicitor, and a man in great trust about him, with a secrett message to be imparted vnto him in his maiesties behalf: which message though it were in deed for *the* time verie secrett, yet fell it out at last to be openly knowne to the worlde, both to the kings great dishonor and perpetuall infamie of the wicked and traiterous

[1] Fol. 89, back.   [2] Fol. 90.

messenger as after shall appeare, neuertheles this messenger beinge come to the presence of this blessed father in his prison, did there his arraut (as it seemed) accordinge to the kings commaundment, for it was not longe after his returne to the kinge with answere of his message, but an indictment of highe treason was framed againſt him, and he arraigned & condemned at the barr vpon the talke that had passed betweene them so secretlie, as after shall be declared vnto you.

[1] It fell out in the meane time that Pope Paul the third of blessed memorie, hearing much of the great constancie of this blessed man, as well before his imprisonment, as now in all the time of his hard restraint, was disposed to advaunce him to a higher dignitie and place accordinge to his great worthines and desert, thinkinge that by reason of this kinde of advauncment the kinge would have shewed him more clemencie, and lefte of further working him trooble and daunger, for his great dignities sake. And so at a solemne creation of Cardinalls had at Rome in the firſt yere of his Consecration, amonge diuers other worthie and famous Cardinalls, this good bishopp was also created a Cardinall the xxjth daie of Maie, in the yere of our Lord god, 1535, intituled Sanctæ ecclesiæ Tituli Sancti vitalis presbiter Cardinalis, whervpon shortly after the Cardinalls hatt was sent towardes him, but when it came to Callis it was there staid till such time as the kinge was aduertised therof, and his pleasure knowne, who (as soone as he heard of yt) [2] sent speedily in great anger to the Lord Deputie, commaunding him in any wise to suffer it to come no nearer till his further pleasure knowne, and immediatly after sent Maiſter Thomas Crumwell, his Secretarie, to this good father in his prison to aduertise him what was done, only to the intent to know what he would saie to yt. Maiſter Crumwell being come into his Chamber, and entring into talke with him of many matters, asked at last, " My lord of Rocheſter " (said he), "yf the Pope should now send you a Cardinalls hatt, what would you doe, would you take yt?" " Sir " (said he), " I know my self farr vnworthie of any such dignitie, that I thinke nothinge leſſe then such matters : but yf he doe send it me, assure your self I will worke with it by all the meanes I can to benefitt the Church of Chriſt, and in that respect I will receive it

[1] Fol. 90, back. [2] Fol. 91.

vpon my knees." Maifter Crumwell making report afterward of this anfwere to the kinge, the kinge faid againe with great indignacion and fpite : " yea, is he yet fo luftie ? Well, let the Pope fend him a hatt when he will, but I will fo provide that when foeuer it commeth he fhall weare it on his fhoulders for head fhall he have none to fett it on."

[1] Wherfore the kinge mindinge now vpon the returne of Rich vnto him, to tract no longer time, feeing he had matter fufficient (as he thought) to condemne him of high treafon for fpeaking againft his new lawes, caufed a Commiffion to be made vnder his great feale to inquire and determine treafons : which Commiffion was dated the firft day of June, in the xxvij[th] yere of his raigne, againft which time the kings learned Councell had alfo drawne an indightment of treafon againft this bleffed byfhopp, and three holy mounkes of the Charter-houfe of London, whofe names were, William Exmew, Humfray Midlemore, and Sabaftian Nudigate. This indightment was not longe in findinge, for on Saint Barnabies daie the Apoftle beinge the xj[th] of June, it was prefented to the Commiffioners fittinge in the kings bench at Weftminfter, whervpon the Carthufians were fhortly after araigned and condemned, and having iudgment of high treafon pronounced vpon them, were moft cruelly put to death at Tyborne, the xix[th] daie of June next followinge, all in their religious habittes : But this good father Bifhop of Rochefter, [2] or rather this devout and moft reuerend Cardinall, of the holy Church of Rome (for fo I may now from henceforth terme him), chaunced at that prefent to be fo fick and feeble that he kept his bedd in great daunger of his life : Wherfore the kinge fent vnto him diuers phifitians to geve him prefervatives, wherby he might the rather be able to come to his publike tryall and cruell punifhment, which the kinge above all things defired, in fo much that he fpent vpon him in charge of phificke the fome of fortie or fiftie poundes : and in the meane time, left any conveiance might be made of his goods remayninge at Rochefter, or els where in Kent, the kinge fent downe Sir Richard Morrifon of his privie chamber, and one Eftwick, with certaine other Commiffioners to make a feifure of all his movable goodes they could

[1] Fol. 91, back.   [2] Fol. 92.

there finde. Thefe Commiffioners being come to Rochefter, accordinge to their commiffion entred his howfe, and firft turned out all his fervants. Then they fell to riflinge of his goodes, wherof fome part was taken to the kings vfe, but more was imbafeled to the vfes of them felves and their fervants. Then they came into his librarie of bookes, which the[y] fpoyled in moft pittifull wife, fcattering them in fuch fort as it was lamentable to behoulde: [1]for it was replenifhed with fuch and fo many kinde of bookes, as the lyke was fcant to be found againe in the poffeffion of any one private man in *Chris*tendome: and of them they truffed vp xxxij great pipes, befides a number that were ftolen awaie. And wheras many yeares before he had made a deede of guifte of all thofe bookes and other his howfehould ftuffe to the Colledge of St. Johns in Cambrige (as is mentioned in the begininge of this Hiftorie), the poore College was now defrauded of their guifte, and all was turned an other waie: And where lykewife a fome of money of three hundred poundes was geven by one of his predifceffors, a bifhopp of Rochefter, to remaine for ever to the faid Sea of Rochefter, in cuftodie of the bifhop for the time beinge, for any fodain mifchance that by occafion might hap vnto the bifhopricke, the fame fome of CCCli, with Cli more laid to yt, was found in his gallerie locked in a Cheft, and from thence carryed cleane awaie by the Commiffioners. Amonge all other things found in his howfe I cannot omitt to tell you of a coffer ftandinge in his Oratorie, where comonly no man came but himfelf alone, for it was his fecret place of praier. This coffer beinge furely locked and ftandinge alwaies [2]fo neere vnto him, every man began to thinke *that* fome great treafure was there ftored vp, wherfore becaufe no collufion or falfehood fhould be vfed to defraude the kinge in a matter of fo great charge as this was thought to be, witneffes were folemnly called to be prefent, fo the coffer was broken vp before them; but when it was open they found within it in fteed of gould and filver, which they looked for, a fhirt of hear and two or three whipps, wherwith he vsed full often to punifh himfelf, as fome of his Chaplins and fervants would report that were then about him, and curioufly marked his doings. And other treafure then that found they none at all. But when report

[1] Fol. 92, back. [2] Fol. 93.

was made to him in his prifon of the opening of that Coffer he was verie forie for yt, and faid that yf haft had not made him forget that and many things els, they fhould not have found yt there at that time.

After this moft reuerend Cardinall was recouered to fome better ftrength by the helpe of his phifitions, and that he was more able to be carryed abroade, he was on Thurfdaie the xvij[th] of June, brought to the kings bench at Weftminfter hall from the towre, with a huge number of halberdes, bills, *and* other weapons, about him, and the Axe of the towre borne before him with the edge from him (as the manner is). And becaufe he was not yet fo well recouered that he was able to walke by land all the waie on foote, he road part of the waie on horfebacke, in a blacke cloath gowne, and the reft he was carried by water, for that he was not able [1] to ride through for weaknes. As foone as he was come to Weftminfter, he was there prefented at the barre before *the* faid Commiffioners, beinge all fet readie in their places againft his cominge, whofe names were thefe : Sir Thomas Awdley, Knight, lord Chauncellor of England ; Charles, Duke of Suffolk ; Henrie, Erle of Cumberlande ; Thomas, Erle of wiltfhire ; Thomas Crumwell ; Sir Iohn Fitz James, cheef Iuftice of England ; Sir Iohn Baldwine, cheefe iuftice of the common pleas ; Sir William Pawlett ; Sir Richard Lyfter, cheefe barron of the Efchequer ; Sir Iohn Port ; Sir Iohn Spilman ; and Sir Walter Luke, Iuftice of the kings bench ; and Sir Anthonie Fitzharbert, one of the Iuftices of the common pleas. Beinge thus prefented before thefe commiffioners, he was commaunded by the name of Iohn Fifher, late of Rochefter, Clerke, otherwife called Iohn Fifher, bifhop of Rochefter, to hould vp his hand, which he did with a moft cheerfull countenance and rare conftancie. Then was his indictment read, which was verie longe and full of wordes, but the effect of it was thus : That he malicioufly, trayteroufly, and falflie, had faid thefe words : " The Kinge our foveraigne lord is not fupreme head in earth of the Church of England : " And beinge reade to the ende it was afked him whether he was guiltie of this treafon or noe ? whervnto he pleaded not guiltie · Then was a Iurie of twelve men (beinge freeholders of

[1] Fol. 93, back.

middlefex) called to trie the yffue, whofe names were thefe: Sir
Hugh Vaughan, Knight; Sir Walter Hungerford, Knight; Thomas
[1] Burbage; Iohn Nudigate; william Browne; Iohn Heues; Iafpar
Leake; Iohn Palmer; Richard Henrie Yonge; Henrie Lodisman;
Iohn Erlerington; and George Heveminghanı, Efquiers. Thefe
twelve men being fworne to trie whether the prifoner were guiltie of
this treafon or noe, at laft came forth to geve evidence againft him,
Mr. Riche, the fecret and clofe meffenger that paffed between the
kinge and him, as you have read before, who openly in the prefence
of the Iudges, and all the people there affembled (which were a
hughe number) depofed and fware that he heard the prifoner faie in
plaine wordes within the towre of London, that he beleeved in his
confcience, and by his learninge affuredly knewe, that the kinge
nether was, nor by right could be, fupreame head in earth of the
Church of England.

When this bleffed father heard the accufacions of this moft
wretched and falfe perfon, contrarie to his former oath and promiffe,
he was not a little aftonied therat, wherfore he faid to him in this
manner: "Maifter Rich, I cannot but marvaile to heare you come in
and beare witneffe againft me of thefe wordes, knowinge in what fecret
manner you came to me; but fuppofe I fo faid vnto you, yet in that
fayinge I committed no treafon: for vpon what occafion and for
what caufe it might be faid your felf doth know right well. And
therfore, beinge nowe vrged" (faid he) " by this occafion to open
fomwhat of this matter, I fhall defire my lordes and others here to
take a litle patience in hearing what I fhall faie for my felf. This
man" (meaninge Maister Rich) "came to me from the king (as he faid)
on a fecret meffage, with commendacions from his grace, [2] declaringe at
large what a good opinion his maieftie had of me, and how forie he
was of my trooble, with many more wordes then are here needfull to
be recited, becaufe they tended fo much to my praife, as I was not
only afhamed to heare them, but alfo knew right well that I could
no waie deferve them. At laft he brake with me of the kings
fupremacie, lately graunted vnto him by acte of perlement, 'to the
which' (he faid), 'although all the bifhops in the realme haue con-

[1] Fol. 94.   [2] Fol. 94, back.

fented, except your felf alone, and alfo the whole Court of Parlement, both fpirituall and temperall, except a verie fewe,' yet he tould me that the king, for better fatiffaccion of his owne confcience, had fent him vnto me in this fecret manner to know my full opinion in the matter, for the great affyaunce he had in me more then in any other. He added further, that yf I would herein franklie and freely advertife his maieftie of my knowledge, that vpon certificat of my miflykinge he was verie lyke to retract much of his former doinges, and make fatiffaccion for the fame, in cafe I fhould fo advife him. When I had heard all his meffage, and confidered a litle vpon his wordes, I put him in minde of the new Act of Parlement, which, ftanding in force as it doth againft all them that fhall directly faie or doe any thing againft yt, might therby indaunger me verie much, in cafe I fhould vtter vnto him any thinge that were offenfive againft the lawe. To that he tould me, that the kinge willed him to affure me on his honor, and in the worde of a kinge, that whatfoeuer I fhould faie vnto him by this his fecrett meffenger, I fhould abide no daunger nor perrill for it, nether that any advantage fhould be taken againft me for the fame: no, although my wordes were never fo directly againft the Statute, feeinge [1] it was but a declaracion of my mind fecretly to him, as to his owne perfon. And for the meffenger himfelf, he gaue me his faithfull promiffe that he would neuer vtter my wordes in this matter to any man livinge, but to the kinge alone. Now therfore, my lordes" (quoth he), " feeinge yt pleafed the kings maieftie to fend me word thus fecretly, vnder the pretence of plaine and trewe meaninge, to know my poor advife and opinion in thefe his waightie and great doinges (which I moft gladly was, and euer will be, to fend him); me thinke it is verie hard in Iuftice to heare the meffengers accufacion, and to alowe the fame as a fufficient teftimonie againft me, in cafe of treafon." To this the meffenger would make no direct anfwere, but with a moft impudent and fhameles face (nether denying his wordes for falfe, nor confeffinge them for trewe) faid, that whatfoeuer he had faid vnto him on the kings behalf, he faid no more then his maieftie commaunded him: " But" (faid he) " yf I had faid to you in fuch fort as you haue declared,

[1] Fol. 95.

I would gladly know what difcharge this is to you in lawe againft his maieftie for fo directly fpeakinge againft the Statute?" wherat fome of the Iudges, taking quick hould one after an other, faid that this meffage or promiffe from the kinge to him nether could nor did, by vigor of the lawe, difcharge him, but in fo declaring of his minde againft the Supremacie, yea, though it were at the kings owne commaundement and requeft, he committed treafon by the Statute and nothinge can difcharge him from death but the kings pardon. This good father, perceaving the fmall [1] account made of his wordes and the favorable credit geven to his accufer, might then eafilie fmell which waie the matter would goe: wherfore, directing his fpeeches to the lordes, his Iudges, he faid: "Yet I praie you, my lordes, confider that by all equitie, iuftice, worldly honeftie, and curteous dealinges, I cannot (as the cafe ftandeth) be directly charged therwith as with treafon, though I had fpoken the wordes in deed, the fame being not fpoken malicioufly, but in the waie of advife and counfell, when it was requefted of me by the kinge himfelf, and that favour the verie wordes of the Statute do geve me, beinge made only againft fuch as fhall malicioufly gainfaie the kinges fupremacie, and none other." To that it was anfwered by fome of the Iudges, that the worde malicioufly in the Statute, is but a superfluous and void word: for if a man fpeake againft the kings fupremacie by any manner of meanes, that fpeakinge is to be vnderftanded and taken in lawe as malicioufly. "My lorde" (faid he), "yf the lawe be fo vnderftood, then it is a hard expofition, and (as I take it) contrarie to the meaninge of them that made the lawe. But then let me demaund this queftion, whether a fingle teftimonie of one man maie be admitted as fufficient to prove me guiltie of treafon for fpeaking thefe wordes, or noe? and whether my anfwere negatively maie not be accepted againft his affirmative, to my [2] availe and benefitt, or noe?" To that the Iudges and lawiers anfwered, that (beinge the kings cafe) it refted much in confcience and difcretion of the Iurie, "and as they vpon the evidence geven before them, fhall find yt, you are ether to be acquited, or els by iudgment to be condemned." The Iurie, havinge heard all this fimple evidence, departed (according to the order) into a

[1] Fol. 95, back.   [2] Fol. 96.

fecret place, there to agree vpon the verdict; but before they went from the place the cafe was fo aggravated to them by my lord Chancellor, making it fo hainous and daungerous a treafon, that they eafily perceived what verdict they muft returne, or els heape fuch daunger vpon their owne heades, as was for none of their cafes to beare. Some other of the Commiffioners charged this moft reverend Cardinall with obftinacie and fingularitie, alleadging that he, beinge but one man, did prefumptuoufly ftand againft that which was in the great Councell of Parliament agreed and finally confented vnto by all the Bifhopps of this Realme, faving himfelf alone. But to that he anfwered, that he might well be accounted finguler, yf he alone fhould ftand in this matter (as they faid); but, having on his part the reft of the bifhopps of Chriftendome, farr furmountinge the number of the bifhops of England, they could not iuftly account him finguler. And having, on his part, all the Catholick bifhops of the world, from Chrift his Affention till nowe, ioyned with the whole confent of Chrifts vniuerfall Church, "I muft needs" (faid he), "account mine owne part farre the furer. And as for obftinacie, which is likewife obiected againft me, I have no waie to [1]cleere my felf therof, but by my owne folemne word *and* promiffe to the contrarie, yf you pleafe to beleeue it; or els, yf that will not ferve, I am here readie to confirme the fame by mine oath." Thus in effect he anfwered their obiections, though with many moe wordes, both wifely and profoundly vttered, and that with marvelous corragious and rare conftancie, in fo much as many of his hearers, yea, fome of his Iudges, lamented fo greevoufly, that their inward forrowe on all fides was expreffed by the outward teares of their eyes, to perceiue fuch a famous and reuerrend man in daunger to be condemned to cruell death by fuch an impious lawe, vpon fo weake evidence geven by fuch a wicked accufer, contrarie to all faith and promiffe of the kinge himfelf. But all pittie, mercie, and right being laid afide, rigor, crueltie and malice, tooke place: for the xij men, beinge fhortly returned from their confultacion, verdict was geven that he was guiltie of *the* treafon: which, although they thus did vpon the menacinge *and* threatninge wordes of the Commiffioners, and the

[1] Fol. 96, back.

kings learned Counfell, yet was it (no doubt) full fore againft their
confciences (as fome of them would after report to their dying daies)
only for fafetie of their goods *and* lives, which they were well aflured
to lofe in cafe they had acquyted him. After the verdict thus geven
by the xij men, The lo*r*d Chancellor, com*m*aunding filence to be kept,
faid vnto the p*r*ifoner in this forte : My lord of Rochefter, you haue
bene here araigned of high treafon, and puttinge yo*ur* felf to the
triall of xij men, you haue pleaded not guiltie, and they, notw*i*th-
ftandinge, have found you guilty in theire confciences : wherefore, y*f*
you haue any more to ¹faie for yo*u*rfelf, you are nowe to be heard,
or els to receive iudgment accordinge to the order and courfe of the
lawe. Then faid this blefled father againe : " Truly, my Lo*rd*s, yf
that which I haue before fpoken be not fufficient, I haue no more to
faie, but only to defire Almightie God to forgeve them that haue
thus condemned me, for I thinke they know not what they haue
done." Then my lo*rd* Chancellor, framinge himfelf to a folemnitie
in countenance, pronounced fentence of death vpon him in manne*r*
and forme followinge : " You fhall be ledd to the place from whence
you came, and from thence fhall be drawne through the Cittie to the
place of execution at Tyborne, where yo*ur* body fhall be hanged by
the necke : and beinge half alive, you fhall be cutt downe and
throwne to the ground, yo*ur* bowells to be taken out of yo*ur* body,
and burnt before you, beinge alive ; yo*ur* head to be fmitten of, and
yo*ur* bodie to be devided into four quarters ; and after, yo*ur* head
and quarters to be fet vp where the kinge fhall appoint, and god
have mercy vpon yo*ur* foule."

After the pronouncing of this horrible and cruell fentence of
death, the Leiftenant of the Towre with his bande of men ftood
readie to receive and carrie him back againe to his prifon. But before
his departure he defired audience of the Com*m*iffione*r*s for a few
wordes, which being graunted he faid thus in effect : " My Lo*r*ds, I
am here condemned before you of high treafon for denyall of *th*e
kings Sup*r*emacie oue*r* the Church of England, but by what order
of iuftice I leave to god, who is fearcher both of *th*e kings maie*j*ties
confcience and yo*ur*s. ²Neue*r*theles beinge found guiltie (as it is

¹ Fol. 97.   ² Fol. 97, back.

tearmed) I am and muſt be content with all that god ſhall ſend, to whoſe will I wholely reſerve and ſubmitt my ſelf. And now to tell you more plainly my minde towching this matter of the king's Supremacie, I thinke in deed and alwais have thought, and do now laſtly affirme, that his Grace cannot iuſtly claime any ſuch Supremacie over the Church of god as he now taketh vpon him, nether hath it bene euer ſeene or heard of, that anie temporall Prince before his daies hath preſumed to that dignitie. wherfore yf the kinge will now adventure himſelf in proceedinge in this ſtraunge and vnwonted Caſe, no doubt but he ſhall deeply incurre the greevous diſpleaſure of Almightie god, to the great daunger of his owne ſoul and of manie others, and to the vtter ruine of this realme committed to his charge : wherof will enſewe ſome ſharpe puniſhment at his hande. wherfore I pray God his grace may remember himſelf in time, and hearken to good Counſell, for the preſervation of himſelf and his realme, and the quietnes of all Chriſtendome ;" Which wordes being ended he was conveyed back againe to the towre of london, part on foote, and part on horſeback, with a lyke number of men bearing halberds and other weapons about him, as was before at his coming to araignment. And when he was come to the towre gate, he turned him back to all his traine that had thus conducted him forward and backward, and ſaid vnto them, "my maiſters, I thanke you all for the great labor and paines ye have taken with me this daie, I am not able to geue you any thinge in recompence, for I have nothinge lefte, and therfore I praie accept in [1]good part my hartie thankes : " and this he ſpake with ſo luſtie a corrage, ſo amiable a countenance, and with ſo freſh and livelie a colour, as he ſeemed rather to haue come from a great feaſt or a banquett, then from his Araignment, ſhewing by all his ieſtures and outward countenance ſuch ioy and gladnes, as it was eaſie to perceave how erneſtly he deſired in his hart to be in that bleſſed ſtate for which he had ſo longe labored ; wherof he made the ſurer account, for that he was thus innocently condemned for Chriſt's Cauſe.

Thus beinge after his Condemnacion the ſpace of foure daies in his priſon, he occupied himſelf in continuall praier moſt fervently, and although he looked daily for death, yet could ye not haue perceived

[1] Fol. 98.

him one whitt difmaide or difquieted thereat, nether in word nor countenance, but ftill continewed his former trade of conftancie and patience, and that rather with a more ioyfull cheere, and free minde then euer he had done before, which appeared well by this Chaunce that I will tell you. There happened a falfe rumor to rife fodenly amonge the people, that he fhould be brought to his execuc*i*on by a certaine daie, whervpon his Cooke that was wonte to dreffe his dinn*er* and carrie it daily vnto him, hearing among others of this execuc*i*on, dreffed him no dinner at all that daie, wherfore at the Cookes next repaire vnto him, he demaunded the caufe why he brought him not his dinn*er* as he was wonte to doe. "S*ir*" (faid *the* Cooke), "it was comonly talked all the towne ou*er* that you fhould haue dyed *that* daie, and therfore I thought it but in vaine to dreffe anie thing for you." "Well," faid he merrily to him againe, "for all that report thou feeft me yet alive, and therfore whatfoeu*er* newes thou fhalt heare of me hereafter, let me no more lacke my dinn*er*, but make yt readie as thou art wont to doe, and yf thou fee me dead when thou co*m*meft, then eat it thyfelf; but I promife thee, yf I be alive, I mind by god's grace to eate neu*er* a bitt the leffe."

[1]Thus while this bleffed Bifhop, and moft reu*er*end Cardinall, lay daily expecting the houre of his death, the king (who no leffe defired his death then himfelf looked for it) caufed at laft a writt of execution to be made, and brought to S*ir* Edmund walfingham, Lieuetenent of the towre. But where by his iudgment at Weftm*in*f*t*er, he was condemned (as ye haue heard before) to drawing, hanginge, and quarteringe, as traytors always be, yet was he fpared from that cruell execuc*i*on, not for any pittie or clemencie ment on the kings part towards him. But the only caufe therof (as I have credibly heard) was for that, yf he fhould have bene laid vpon a hardell and drawne to Tyborne, being *t*he ordinarie place for that purpofe, and diftant above two miles from *t*he Towre, it was not vnlykely, but he would have bene deade longe ere he had come there, feeing he was a man of great age, and befides *tha*t verie fickly and weake of body, through his longe imprifonment. wherfore order was taken that he fhould be ledd noe further then to the Towre hill, and there to have his heade ftrooke of.

[1] Fol. 98, back.

After the Leiftennant had received this bloodie writte, he called vnto him certaine perfons, whofe fervice and prefence was to be ufed in that bufines, commaunding them to be readie againft the next day in the morninge, and becaufe it was then verie late in the night, and the prifoner afleepe, he was loath to diffeafe him from his reft for that time, and fo in the morninge before five of the Clocke he came to him in his chamber in the bell towre, finding him yet afleepe in his bedd, and waked him, fhewing him that he was come to him on a meffage from the kinge ; and after fome circumftances [1] vfed with perfwafion that he fhould remember himfelf to be an ould man, and that for age he could not by courfe of nature live longe ; he tould him at the laft that he was come to fignifie vnto him, that the king's pleafure was he fhould fuffer death that forenoone. " Well " (quoth this bleffed father), " yf this be your errand, you bringe me no great newes, for I have longe time looked for this meffage ; and I moft humbly thanke the kings majeftie that it pleafeth him to ridd me from all this worldly bufines, and I thank you alfo for your tydings. But I praie you, maifter Leivetennant" (faid he), " when is my houre that I muft goe hence?" "Your houre" (faid the leivetennant), "muft be nine of the clocke." "And what houre is it now?" faid he. "Yt is now about five," faid the Leivetenant. "Well, then" (faid he), "let me by your patience fleepe an houre or two, for I have flept verie little this night ; and yet, to tell you the truth, not for any feare of death, I thanke god, but by reafon of my great infirmitie and weaknes." " The kings further pleafure is " (faid the Leivetennant), "that you fhould vfe as litle fpeech as may be, fpecially of any thing towchinge his Maieftie, wherby the people fhould have any caufe to thinke of him or his proceedings otherwife then well." " for that " (faid he), " you fhall fee me order myfelf as, by god's grace, nether the king nor any man els fhall have occafion to miftake of my wordes : " with which anfwere the Leivetenant departed from him, and fo the prifoner falling againe to reft flept foundly two houres and more. And after he was waked he called to his man to helpe him vp. But firft of all he commaunded him to fetch awaie the fhirte of heare which accuftomably he wore on his backe, and to convey it

[1] Fol. 99.

privily out of the howſe, and in ſtedd therof to laie him out a cleane
white ſhirt, and all the beſt apparrell he had as cleanly bruſhed as
might be, and as he was in araying himſelf, his man, perceavinge in
him a more curioſtie and care for the fine *and* cleanly [1] wearinge of
his apparrell that day then eue*r* was wont to be before, demaunded
of him what this ſodaine change ment, ſaying that his lordſhip knew
well ynough he muſt put of all againe within two houres and looſe
yt. "What of that?" (ſaid he); "doſt thou not marke that this is our
mariage daie, and that it behooveth vs therfore to vſe more clenlineſſe
for ſolemnitie of *th*at mariage?" About nine of the Clocke the
Leiuete*n*nant came againe to his priſon, and finding him almoſt readie
ſaid that he was now come for him. "I will waite vpon you
ſtraight" (ſaid he), "as faſt as this thinne bodie of mine will geve
me leave." Then ſaid he to his man, "reach me my furred tippett
and put it about my necke." "O, my lord," quoth the Leiuetenant,
"what need you be ſo carefull for yo*ur* health for this litle, being as
yo*ur* lordſhip knoweth not much above an houre?" "I thinke no
otherwiſe" (ſaid this bleſſed father), "but yet in *th*e meane time I
will keepe myſelf as well as I can till the verie time of my execuci*o*n:
for I tell you truth, though I have (I thanke our lord) a verie good
deſire and willing minde to die at this p*r*eſent, and ſo truſt of his
infinite mercie and goodnes he will continewe it, yett will I not
willingly hinder my health in the meane time one minute of an
houre, but ſtill prolonge the ſame as longe as I can by ſuch reaſonable waies and meanes as Almighty god hath provided for me." And
with that, taking a litle booke in his hand, which was a new Teſta-
ment lying by him, he made a croſſe on his foreheade and went out
of his priſon doare with the Leiuetenant; [2] being ſo weake that he
was ſcant able to goe downe *th*e ſtairs, wherfore at the ſtaires foote,
he was taken vp in a chaire between two of the Leiuetenants men,
and carried to the towre gate with a great number of weapons about
him to be deliue*r*ed to the Sheriffes of London for execution. And
as they were come to the vttermoſt precinct or libertie of the towre,
they reſted there with him a ſpace, till ſuch time as one was ſent
afore, to know in what redines the Sheriff*es* were to receiue him;

[1] Fol. 99, back.   [2] Fol. 100.

duringe which fpace he rofe out of his chair, and ftandinge on his
feete leaned his fhoulder to the wall, and lifting his eyes vp toward
heaven he opened his litle booke in his hand and faid, "O lord, this
is the laft time that eu*er* I fhall open this booke, let fome comfortable
place now chaunce vnto me, wherby I, thy poore fervant, maie glorifie
thee in this [m]y [1] laft howre," and with that, lookinge into the booke,
the firft thinge that came to his fight, were thefe wordes, "*hec est autem
vita eterna vt cognofcant te folum ver*u*m deum, et quem mififti Jefum
Chriftum. Ego te clarificaui fuper terram opus confum*mavi quod
dedisti mihi vt faciam: et nunc clarifica tu me pater apud temetipfum
claritate quam habui priufquam*, etc." And with that he fhutt the
booke together and faid: "Here is even learning ynough for me even
to my lives ende." And fo (the Sherifs being readie for him) he was
taken vp againe amonge certaine of the Sheriffs men with a new and
much greater companie [2] of weapons then was before, and carryed to
the Scaffolde on the towre hill, otherwife called eaft Smithfield, himfelf praying all the waie, and recording vpon the wordes wh*i*ch he
before had read, and when he was come to the foot of the fcaffolde
they that carried him offered to helpe him vp the ftaires; but then
faid he, "Naie, maifters, feeinge I am come fo farre let me alone,
and ye fhall fee me fhifte for myfelf well ynough," and fo went vp
the ftaires without any helpe fo lively, that it was marvaile to them
that knewe before of his debillitie and weaknes. But as he was
mounting vp the ftaires the fowtheaft fonne fhyned verie bright in his
face; whervpon he faid to himfelf thefe wordes, liftinge vp his handes,
"*Accedite ad eum et illuminamini et facies veſtræ non confundentur.*"
By that time he was vp the Scaffold, it was about tenn of the Clocke,
where the executioner being readie to doe his office kneeled downe to
him (as the fafhion is) and afked him forgevenes. "I forgeve thee,"
faid he, "with all my harte, and I truft thou fhalt fee me ouercome
this ftorme luftily." Then was his gowne and typpett taken from
him, and he ftood in his dubblett and hofe in fight of all the people;
wherof was noe fmall number affembled to fee this horrible execution.
There was to be feene, a longe, leane, and flender body, having on
it litle other fubftance befides the fkynne and bones, in fo much as

[1] MS. thy.   [2] Fol. 100, back.

moſt part of the beholders marveled much to ſee a living man ſo farr conſumed, for he ſeemed a verie Image of death, and as it were death in man's ſhape vſinge a man's voice, and therefore [1] monſtrous was it thought, that the kinge could be ſo cruell as to put ſuch a man to death, being alreadie ſo neere death as he was, yea, though he had bene an offender in deed. And ſurely it maie be thought that yf he had bene in the Turkes dominion and there found guiltie of ſome great offence; yet would the Turke neuer have put him to death, beinge alreadie ſo neere death. For it is an horrible and exceeding crueltie to kill that thing which is preſently dyinge, except it be for pittie ſake, to ridd it from longer paine; which in this Caſe appeared not, and therfore it maie be thought that the crueltie and hard hart of kinge Henrie in this point, paſſed all the Turkes and Tyrauntes that ever haue bene heard or read of.

When the innocent and holie Cardinall was come vpon the Scaffold, he ſpake to the people in effect as followeth: "Chriſtian people, I am come hither to die for the faith of Chriſts holy Catholick Church, and I thanke god hitherto my ſtomack hath ſerved me verie well thervnto, ſo that yet I have not feared death: wherfore I do deſire you all to helpe and affiſt me with your praiers, that at the verie point and inſtant of deaths ſtroake, I maie in that verie moment ſtand ſtedfaſt without faintinge in any one point of the Catholick faith free from any feare; and I beſeech almightie god of his infinite goodnes to ſave the kinge and this Realme, and that it maie pleaſe him to holde his holy hand ouer yt, and ſend the king good Counſell." Theſe or lyke wordes he ſpake with ſuch a cheerfull countenance, ſuch a ſtowte and conſtant courage, and ſuch a reverent gravitie that [2] he appeared to all men not only void of feare but alſo gladd of death. Beſides this he vttered his wordes ſo diſtinctly and with ſo lowde and cleere a voice, that the people were aſtonied therat, and noted it for a miraculous thinge to heare ſo plaine and audible a voice come from ſo weake and ſickly an ould bodie; for the yongeſt man in that preſence, being in good and perfect health, could not have ſpoken to be better heard and perceived than he was. Then after theſe fewe wordes by him vttered, he kneeled downe on both

[1] Fol. 101.   [2] Fol. 101, back.

his knees and faid certaine praiers, amonge which (as fome reported) one was the Hymne of *Te deum laudamus* to the end, *and t*he pfalme *In te domine fperaui*. Then came the executioner & bound a hand-carcher about his eyes, and fo this holy father lifting up his handes and hart to heaven, faid a few praiers *which* were not longe but fervent and devout, which being ended, he laid his holy head downe over the middeft of the blocke, where the Executione*r* being readie with a fharp and heavie Axe cutt a funder his flender necke at one blowe, which bledd fo abundantly that many wonndred to fee fo much blood yffue out of fo leane and flender a bodie; and fo head and body being fevered, his innocent foule mounted to *th*e bliffull ioys of heaven.

And as concerninge the head the Executione*r* put it into a bagge, and carryed it awaie with him, meaninge to have fet it vpon London bridge that night as he was commanded. But it was reported that the ladie Ann Bullen, who was the cheef caufe of this holy mans death, had a certaine defire [1] to fee the head before yt were fett vp; whervpon being brought vnto her, fhe beheld yt a fpace, and at laft contemptuoufly faid thefe or lyke wordes: "Is this head that fo often exclaymed againft me? I truft it fhall neue*r* do me more harme;" and with that ftrykinge it vpon the mouth with the backe of her hand, hurte one of her fingers vpon a tooth that ftood fomwhat more out then the reft did: which finger after grewe fore, *and* puttinge her to paine many daies after, was neue*r*theleffe cured at laft with fome difficultie. But after it was healed the marke of the hurt place remayned to be feene till her dyinge day. This maie feem ftrange, as a rare example of cruell bouldnes in that fexe, which by nature is fearfull and cannot well behould fuch fpectacles, and therfore argues no doubt a wonderfull malice, which fhe by lykelyhood bare to the holy man living, that could thus cruelly vfe his head beinge dead: Then ftrippinge the bodie out of his fhirte and all his cloathes, he departed thence, leavinge the headles carcaffe naked vpon the fcaffold, where it remained after that fort for the moft part of that daie, savinge that one for pittie and humanitie caft a litle ftrawe vpon his privities; and about eight of the clock in the eveninge, com-

[1] Fol. 102.

maundment came from the kings Counfell, to fuch as watched about the dead bodie (for it was ftill watched with manie halberds and weapons), that they fhould caufe it to be buried. Whervpon two of the watchers tooke it vpon a halbert betweene them, and fo carried it to a church yard there hard by, called Allhallows Barkinge, where on the north fide of the Church hard by the wall they digged a grave with their halberdes, and therin without any reuerence tumbled the bodie of this holy prelate and [1] bleffed Martyr all naked and flatt vpon his bellie, without ether fheet or other accuftomed thinge belonging to a chriftian mans buriall, and fo covered it quickly with earth, followinge herein the kings commaundment, who willed it fhould be buryed contemptuoufly. And this was done on the daie of St. Albane the prothomartyr and firft martyr of Englande, being Tuefday the xxij[th] of Iune, in the yere of our redemtion 1535, and the xxvij[th] yere of king Henries raigne, after he had lived full three-fcore and fixteene yeares nyne mounthes and odd daies.

The next daie after his buriall, the head beinge fomwhat per-boyled in hott water, was pricked vpon a pole and fett on high vpon London bridge, amonge the reft of the holy Carthufians heades that suffred death lately before him. And here I cannot omitt to declare vnto you the miraculous fight of this head, which after it had ftand vp the fpace of xiiij daies vpon the bridge could not be perceived to waft nor confume, nether for the weather, which then was verie hott, neither for the parboylinge in hott water, but grewe daily frefher and frefher, fo that in his life time he neuer looked fo well; for his cheekes being bewtifyed with a comly redd, the face looked as though it had beholden the people paffinge by, and would have fpoken to them, which many tooke for a miracle [2] that Almightie god was pleafed to fhew aboue the courfe of nature in thus pre-fervinge the frefh and lively color of his face farr paffinge the color he had beinge alive, wherby was notifyed to the worlde the inno-cencie and holines of this bleffed father, that thus innocently was contented to loofe his head in defence of his mothers heade, the holy Catholick Church of Chrift. Wherfore the people cominge daily to fee this ftrange fight, the paffage ouer the bridge was fo ftopped

[1] Fol. 102, back.   [2] Fol. 103.

with their goinge and cominnge, that almoſt nether Cart nor horſe could paſſe: And therfore at the end of xiiij daies the Executioner commaunded to throwe downe the heade in the night time into the river of Thames, and in place therof was ſett the head of the moſt bleſſed and conſtant Martyr Sir Thomas Moore, his companion and fellowe in all his troobles; who ſuffred his paſſion the vjth day of Julye next followinge.

And towchinge the place of his buriall in Barkinge Church yard, it was well obſerved at that time by diuers worthie parſonages of the nations of Italie, Spaine, and Fraunce, that were then abidinge in the realme, and more dilligently noted and wrote the courſe of things, and with leſſe feare and ſuſpition then any of the kings ſubiects might or durſt doe: that for the ſpace of vij yeares after his buriall there grewe nether leafe nor graſſe vpon his grave, but the earth ſtill remained as bare as though it had bene continewally occupied and trodden.

[1] When by common fame this bloodie execution was blowne and ſpredd abroad, ſtraight waie the name of kinge Henrie began to growe odious amonge all good people, not only in his owne Realme at home, but alſo amonge all forraine princes and nations abroad through Chriſtendome, which ſpecially appeared in the moſt worthie Pope Paule the third, who with great greefe ſignified this horrible and barbarous crueltie by his feuerall letters to the Chriſtian princes, openly deteſtinge the outrage of kinge Henrie in committing ſuch a wicked and manifeſt inurie, not only againſt the freedome and priveledge of the Church of Rome, but alſo againſt the whole ſtate of Chriſtes vniverſall Church, for the which, in ſhort ſpace after, he pronounced the tirrible ſentence of excommunication againſt him.

Lykewiſe the moſt noble and Chriſtian Emperor Charles the vth, at ſuch time as Sir Thomas Moore was beheaded, and word therof brought to him, he ſent ſpeedily for Sir Thomas Elliott, the kings Ambaſſador, there reſident with him, and aſked him whether he heard any ſuch newes or noe; who anſwered him that he heard noe ſuch thinge. [2] "Yea" (ſaid the Emperour), "it is trewe, and too true that Sir Thomas Moore is now executed to death as a good

---

[1] Fol. 103, back. [2] Fol. 104.

Biſhopp hath lately bene before;" and with that (geving a figth) ſaid: "Alas, what ment the kinge to kill two ſuch men : for" (ſaid he) "the Biſhopp was ſuch a one, as for all purpoſes (I thinke) the kinge had not the lyke againe in all his Realme, nether yet was to be matched through Chriſtendome; So that" (said he) "the king, your maiſter, hath (in killinge that Biſhopp) killed at one blowe all the biſhoppes in England," meaning (no doubt) that this biſhop, conſidering his paſtorall care and conſtant profeſſion of his biſhoply duty in defence of the Church, in reſpect of the reſt of his brethren, did only deſerve the name of a biſhopp. "And Sir Thomas Moore" (ſaid he) "was well knowne for a man of ſuch profound wiſdome, cunninge, and vertue, that yf he had bene towards me as he was towardes the kinge your maiſter, I had rather have loſt the beſt Cittie in all my dominion then ſuch a man."

And in lyke manner kinge Frauncis, the french kinge, though in ſome reſpects a man wiſhed to be otherwiſe then he was, yet talkinge on a time with Sir John wallop, the kings Ambaſſador, of thoſe two bleſſed men, tould him plainly that ether the kinge his maiſter had verie ill counſell about him, or els himſelf had a verie hard hart, that could put to death two ſuch worthie men, as the lyke were not again within his realme: wherof kinge Henrie being aduertiſed tooke it verie ill at the hands of king Frauncis for ſo reporting of him, ſayinge, that he did nothinge but that himſelf was firſt made privie to yt.

[1] But generally amonge all Chriſten people kinge Henrie was both ill thought and ill ſpoken of, as no doubt but there was great cauſe, for ſundrie conſideracions, as well for the innocent death of this bleſſed father as of diuers other bleſſed men, both ſpirituall and temperall: wherof ſome dyed before him and ſome after him, though in all reſpects no one comparable to him, partly for his great age, partly for his profound learninge, partly for his ſanctitie of life, and partly for his great and high dignities. as after ſhall be declared unto you.

In ſtature of bodie he was tall and comly, exceeding the common and midle ſort of men: for he was to the quantitie of 6 foote in

[1] Fol. 104, back.

height, and being therwith verie flender and leane, was neuertheles
vpright and well framed, ftraight backed, bigg ioynted and ftrongly
fynewed. His hear by nature black, though in his later time,
through age and imprifonment, turned to hoarenefs or rather white-
nes, his eyes longe and rounde, nether full black nor full graie, but
of a mixt color between both; his forehead fmooth and large, his
nofe of a good and even proportion, fomwhat wide mouthed and
bigg iawed, as one ordained to vtter fpeech much, wherin was notwithftandinge a certaine comlineffe; his fkinne fomwhat tawnie
mixed with manie blew vaines; his face, handes, and all his bodie fo
bare of flefh as is almoft incredible, which came the rather (as may
be thought) [1] by the great abftinance and pennance he vfed vpon
himfelf many yeres together, even from his youth. In his countenance he bare fuch a reuerend gravitie, and therwith in his doings
exercifed fuch difcreet feveritie, that not only of his equalls, but
even of his fuperiors he was both honored and feared. In fpeech
he was verie milde, temperat, and modeft, faving in matters of god
and his charge, which then began to trooble the worlde; and therin
he wolde be earneft above his accuftomed order. But vainly or
without caufe he would neuer fpeake, nether was his ordinarie talke
of common worldly matters, but rather of the Divinitie and high
power of god; of the ioys of heaven and the paines of hell; of the
glorious death of martirs, and ftreight lyfe of Confeffors, with fuch
lyke vertuous and profitable talke, which he alwais vttered with
fuch a heavenly grace, that his wordes were alwais a great edifyinge
to his hearers. He had fuch a continewall impreffion of death in
his hart, that his mowth neuer ceafed to vtter the inward thoughts
of his minde, not only in all times of his exercife, but alfo at his
meales; for he would alwaies faie that the remembrance of death
came neuer out of feafon. And of his owne death he would now
and then (as occafion of fpeech was geven) caft out fuch wordes
as though he had fome foreknowledge of the manner of his
death. For divers of his Chaplens and howfehould fervants have
reported that longe before his death they haue heard him fay that
he fhould not die in his bedd; but alwais in fpeaking therof he

[1] Fol. 105.

would vtter his wordes with fuch a cheerfull countenance [1] as they might eafily perceiue him rather to conceiue ioy then forrowe therat. In ftudie he was verie laborious, and painfull, in preachinge affiduous, euer beating downe herefie *and* vice; in praier moft fervent and devout; in fafting, abftinence, and punifhing of his bare bodie, rigorous without meafure. And generally in all things belonginge to the care and charge of a trew bifhopp, he was to all the bifhops of England living in his daies the verie mirrour *and* lanterne of light. In his time he wrote many famous *and* learned workes, wherof fo manie as haue come to our knowlege I have thought good to notifie vnto you.

(The list of books is omitted, and a note in the margin says: "here wants *the* catalogue of books.")

[2] Many other learned treatifes this profound Doctour wrote with great dilligence, wherof no more came to light, becaufe he lived not to finifh them; but my felf have feene divers of them, and fome others I have heard of by report of good and credible perfons. And it was once tould me by a reuerend father, that was Deane of Rochefter many yeares together, named M*aifte*r Phillips, That on a time in the daies of kinge Edward the fixt, when certaine Com*m*iffioners were coming towards him to fearch his howfe for books, he for feare burned a large volume, which this holy bifhop had compiled, contayning in yt the whole ftorie and matter of divorce, which volume he gave him with his owne hand a litle before his trooble for the loffe wherof the deane wold manie times after lament, and wifh the booke whole againe, vpon condicion that he had not one groat to live on. Many other of his workes were confumed by the iniquitie of hereticks, which fhortly after his death fwarmed thick in euery place, and grew into great credit, doing therby what themfelves lifted. And, as it hath bene reported by a good ould preift, called m*aifte*r Buddell, who in his youth wrote many of his books for him, ther came to him on a certaine time, in the fore faid king Edwards daies, a minifter, by authoritie of him that then occupyed the Sea of Rochefter, and tooke from him as many written bookes and papers of this holy mans labors as loaded a horfe, and, carrying them to his m*aifte*r, they were all afterwards burned (as he heard faie) by *the*

[1] Fol. 105, back.   [2] Fol. 106.

ma*ift*er minifter *and* t*h*e man. [1] This ma*ift*er Buddell was then Parfon of Cookeftone, in kent, not far from Rochefter, where he yet liveth a verie ould man, and declareth many notable things of the aufterio life and vertue of this holy man.

But, although many of his doings were thus obfcured and loft by this wicked meane, yet fhall his name neu*er* die, nor be darkned, fo longe as the reft of his writings fhall remaine, nor yet fo longe as the worthie wrytings of fo many other profound Doctors fhall be extant, which after his daies wrote highlie to his laude and praife: wherof, although the number be verie great, and would require a whole volume to expreffe them all, yet I cannot omitt to fet forth vnto you the fayings of fome of them, beinge as they are of fuch great authoritie, credit, and worthines.

And, firft to begin at our holy Father, Pope Paule the third, he, wryting (as before is faid) to the Princes of *Chrift*endome, of the moft wicked and cruell dealinge of kinge Henrie againft this godlie man, wrote amonge others one letter to Ferdinando, kinge of Romans, which myfelf have feene and redd. In this letter, after great complaint made of kinge Henrie for killing of fuch a man, whom he before for his great fanctitie and vertue had inrolled into the number and focietie of the Cardinalls, hoping therby that all fhould have turned to his better fafetie *and* deliverance, becaufe that dignitie in all places hath ever bene accounted for holy, yet now falling out otherwife; [2] he taketh occafion to compare the doings of king Henrie the eight to the doings of his progenitors, king Henrie the feconde: and this holy father he compareth, or rather preferreth, to the holy martyr, Sa*int* Thomas of Canterburie, fayinge *that* this king Henrie did not only renewe the impietie of that king Henrie, but alfo went far beyond him: for where he flewe one, this flew many. Sa*int* Thomas defended the right of one particuler Church, this of the vniu*er*fall Church: That kinge killed an archbifhopp, but this kinge hath pu to death a Cardinall of the holy Church of Rome. That kinge exiled Sa*int* Thomas by longe banifhment, but this kinge tormented this holie man by long and hard imprifonment. He fent vnto Sa*int* Thomas certaine hired men to kill him: to this was affigned only a hangman.

[1] Fol. 106, back.   [2] Fol. 107.

He caufed S*ai*nt Thomas to be flaine by a forcible death, but this by a fhamefull torment hath killed the holy man of god. He, in conclufion, fought to purge himfelf before Alexander the third, and layinge the falte vpon others, did with humilitie take vpon him fuch pennance as was to him inioyned by the Bifhop of Rome. But this, with a moft obftinat minde, defended his owne horrible fact, fhowing with a moft erneft defire himfelf not only vnwilling to pennance, but alfo becometh a ftubborne and rebellious enemie againft the Church of Rome.

Then confider what that man of happie memorie, Cardinal Poole, wryteth of him in fundrie places of his workes, who in his life time both knewe him, and was familiarly acquainted with him. But fpecially in that booke which he wrote [1] to kinge Henrie the eight intituled *Pro ecclefiafticæ vnitatis defenfione*, wherin he extolleth the name of this bleffed Prelate with wordes accordinge to his great worthines, fayinge to the kinge, that yf an ambaffador had bene to be fent from earth to Heaven, there could not amonge all the Bifhopps and Clergie fo fitt a man be chofen as he; for what other man, faith he, have *the* prefent, or of many yeres paft haue ye had comparable with him in fanctitie, learninge, wifdome, and carefull dilligence in the office and dutie of a bifhop? of whom ye may iuftly above all other nations glorie and reioyce: that if all the corners of Chriftendome were narrowly fought, there could not be found out any one man that in all things did accomplifh the partes and degrees of a bifhopp equall with him. Further, in the fame place he lawdeth him highly for his great travell *and* care in the educac*i*on of youth, fpecially of the yonger students in the vniuer*f*itie of Cambrige, for that by his only meane and motion that noble and right vertuous Ladie Margaret, Counteffe of Richmound and Darbie, fomtime his M*iftrefs*, erected two famous Colleges in the vniuer*f*itie (as before in this Hiftorie hath bene declared) wherin yonge fchollers receive great comfort towards their inftrucc*i*on in learninge: vnto which number himfelf became alfo a patron and father. [2] And, beinge after chofen by the whole confent of *the* vniuer*f*itie, to the roome of their high Chauncellor, he became no

[1] Fol. 107, back.   [2] Fol. 108.

leſſe carefull over them then over the flocke of his Dioceſſe. All which, with manie other high praiſes, this moſt vertuous, learned, and noble borne Cardinall, fetteth out very bountifully of him.

Lykewiſe, bleſſed Sir Thomas Moore, his Companion and fellow in aduerſitie and trooble, vpon occaſion of talke miniſtred vnto him by his daughter, Miſtris Roper, about refuſinge the Oath: by my lord of Rocheſter and himſelf, ſaith in a certaine epiſtle written to ſaid daughter, that he hath him in ſuch a reuerrend eſtimacion, as for his wiſdome, learning, and longe approved vertue together, he reckoneth in this realme noe one man to be matched or compared with him.

Furthermore, the renouned biſhopp of Nuceria, and moſt eloquent Hyſtoriographer of our time, Paulus Jovius; although he lacketh no commendacion of him through his whole Hiſtorie, yet in one place ſpecially he ſaith: that vpon the acceptance of his great charge of a biſhoprick, he became ſo vigilant over his flocke the ſpace of many yeres together, that he was to be woundred at, [1] not only of his owne countrie people at home, but alſo of all other outward nations: then he greatly reuerrenceth him for his conſtant pietie in defendinge the maryage between kinge Henrie and his lawfull wife Queene Catherin, and for withſtandinge the kings wilfull minde in takinge vpon him ſo abſurdly the name and tytle of ſupreame head of the church, for the which he did not refuſe, even in his ould age, to ſuffer the loſſe of libertie, livings, lyfe, and all.

Then waighe what is ſaid of him by that moſte eloquent and learned father of our daies, Staniſlaus Hoſius, biſhopp of Warmia in Poland, and Cardinall of Rome, in his Booke of Confutacion againſt Brentius the Hereticke. His wordes beinge thus: *fatemur et nos Brenti, etc.*; wherein he ſheweth verie notably howe, although in all ages Heretickes haue liſte vp themſelves againſt the Church of god, yet hath he not forſaken or lefte her deſtitute at any time, nether doth he yet forſake her at this daie. For againſt Arrius god raiſed thoſe notable and excellent men, Liberius, Athanaſius, *and* Hillarius. when Macedonius ſpronge, he brought into the feild againſt him, Damaſus, Gregorius Nazianzenus and Baſilius. At an other time Neſtorius

---

[1] Fol. 108 back.

brake out, againſt him were ſent, Celeſtinus, biſhop of Rome, and Cirillus, Archbiſhop of Alexandria. Then yſſued out (I wott not from what dungeon) the Hereticke Eutiches, againſt whom he ſet *the* ſtrong *and* mightie Leo. [1]Lykewiſe Ireneus againſt Valentinus; Tertulian againſt Martian; Origen againſt Celſus; Ciprian againſt Novatus; S*ain*t Jerom againſt Helvidius, Jovinianus, Vigilantius, *and the* luciferans; St. Auguſtine againſt the donatiſts and Pellagians; Agatho againſt the monothelits; Taraſius againſt the Icomomians; Lanfrank, Sirmond and Alger againſt Beringarius; Petrus Clinacenſis againſt *the* Henricians and Petrobruſſians; S*ain*t Bernard againſt Adelherdus. And gene*r*ally, in what time ſoeu*er* hereſies have ſhewed forth their hornes, there have alwais bene by the ſinguler benefit of god, ſuch worthie men for witt, learninge, *and* eloquence as have confuted them, partly by authoritie of ſcriptures, and partly by tradition of the Church. Nether hath god in theſe our vnfortunate daies, failed his church; for wheras you Lutherans are broken forth, and from you are ſprunge Zwinglians, Munncerans or Patrimontanes, and a number of horrible ſects of hereticks moe; god hath produced againſt you into the battell many worthie men indewed with ſinguler witt and excellent learninge, by whom yo*ur* raginge madnes might be suppreſſed *and* put downe: Amonge whom ſpecially and by name, was that famous holy man, John Fyſher, biſhop of Rocheſter, who in defence of the faith and catholick church of Ch*r*iſt, neuer ſtoock for the loſſe of his life and ſheedinge of his blood.

[2]Finally, whoſoeu*er* ſhall reade the workes of Cocleus wiſellius, Eckius, and others, learned writers of Germanie; of the worthie biſhop and eloquent wryter, Oſorius; of Alphonſus de Caſtro, and others of Spaine and of Portugall; beſides a number of ſuch other learned fathers of many nations, wherof ſome lived in his owne daies, and ſome ſince, ſhall eaſily perceiue that he was a man, for his profound learninge and rare vertue, highly reue*r*renced and eſteemed throughout Ch*r*iſtendome.

And, no doubte, but yf his writings and doings be well compared, ye ſhall find him moſt lyke vnto thoſe holy fathers and

[1] Fol. 109.   [2] Fol. 109, back.

Doctors that in the primative Church, laid the very firft ground and foundacion of our beleef, vpon *the* which we haue fince refted and ftaid our felues: whom to difcribe wholely and fully vnto you according to his worthines, I will not take vpon me, nether am I able to do it. No, were I as eloquent as Cicero, or as wittie and fubtill as Ariftotle, as copious as Demofthenes, or as p*ro*found in philofophie as Plato: fuch, and fo innumerable, were his finguler vertues. But herin I will content myfelf with the gen*er*all commendac*i*ons which all the famous vniuer*fi*ties of Diuinitie in Europe do geve this learned bifhopp, calling him bleffed Martyr, and aleadginge his workes for great authoritie.

[1] Thus much I may alfo faie, that vnto Iuftus his pr*e*deffeffor, the firft bifhop of Rochefter, he was a iuft and true fucceffor. The place of his birth he doth greatly bewtifie, with *the* glorious bifhopp, S*ain*t John of Beue*r*ley. To the countrie of kente, where he was bifhopp, he is an ornament w*ith* S*ain*t Thomas of Canterburie. In gravitie of his wrytinge he is to be reue*r*renced with faint Bede; for ftowt defendinge the right and libertie of the holy Church againft the power of princes, he is not inferior to the bleffed bifhopp S*ain*t Ambrofe and S*ain*t Chrifoftome. In prayinge for his enemies and perfecutors he refembleth holy S*ain*t Stephen. In conftancie and ftowtnes of his martirdome he was a feconde Cyprian. But, above all others, he is moft to be lykened and compared to that holy prophett and martyr of god, S*ain*t John Baptift. And firft, to fet a fide the congruence in their names of John, it is to be noted, that as that John lived in wildernes a hard and folitarie life, in pennance and punifhment of himfelf, so this John lived a folitarie and auftere life in his private howfe and Cell (faving when he was called abroade to other bufines), punifhing himfelf w*ith* ftudie, hard lodginge vpon the matts, faftinge, prayinge, wearing of haire fhirtes, and whippinge himfelf. Lykewife, as that John preached dilligently the co*m*minge of Chrift at hande, gevinge knowledge of falvation to all them that would beleeue and be baptifed. So this John, with lyke dilligence and care warned *the* people by his continewall prechinge and wrytinge of Chriftes departure at hand, in cafe they ftopped not

[1] Fol. 110.

their eares againft thofe horrible herefies daily [1]preached and fet forth vnto them. And as that John dyed for a cafe of matrimonie, fayinge to kinge Herod: It is not lawfull for thee to have thy brothers wife. So this John dyed for a Case in matrimonie, contrarie in apparance, but agreeable in fubftance and truth, faying vnto kinge Henrie: It is not lawfull for thee to put awaie thy wife and take an other, though fhe were once thy brothers wife, feeinge thy brother is dead without yffue, and thou nowe lawfully maryed vnto her by difpenfacion and authoritie of the Church. for Herod (whom Saint John Baptift reprehended) tooke to him his brothers wife, his brother livinge, which (as manifeftly repugning to gods lawe) could not be done. But kinge Henrie tooke his brothers wife when his brother was dead, without yffue of her, which by Moyfes law is not in that Cafe forbidden, and by the authoritie of the Church may be permitted, as this was: and therefore was the mariage good and lawfull, and confequently the fecond, deteftable and vnlawfull. furthermore, as that Johns heade was begged of kinge Herod at a banquett, by a pfaltreffe or woman dauncer, so this Johns head was begged by a lyke perfon of kinge Henrie, as he fate banquettinge and cheeringe at his howfe of Hanworth. As that John was beheaded on the birth daie of kinge Herod, fo this John was beheadded on the birth daie of kinge Henrie, the kinge having that day accomplifht the iuft age of five and fortie yeres. [2]And as the holy finger of that John, which pointed to the lambe when he faid "Ecce agnus dei," was miraculoufly preferved from corruption longe after his death and martyrdome, fo the holy head of this John wherwith he ftowtly defended the head of our holy mother the Church, was by miracle preferved longe after his martyrdome with a frefh and lively colour, till by commaundment of the kinge it was taken away and conveyed out of fight. finally, as in the perfon of that John there dyed 3 notable functions or offices at once, That is to faie, of a preift, a prophett, and a patriarke, fo in the perfon of this John there dyed 3 lyke worthie vocacions, That is to fay, a preift, a Bifhop, and a Cardinall. And thus we fee how the death of our holy John may be compared to Saint John Baptifts death.

[1] Fol. 110, back.   [2] Fol. 111.

And, yet in verie deed, for fome refpects it furpaffeth the death of Saint John; and the wicked doings of kinge Henrie furpaffeth lykewife the wicked doings of kinge Herod. for Saint John Baptift reprehended Herod, and would not alowe his Acte in taking only his brothers wife, but kinge Henrie (whom this, our holy John, reprehended) put awaie his lawfull and vertuous wife, and tooke to him (as is rehearfed) his owne vnlawfull daughter, made fure alreadie to another, and in honeftie no better then an harlott. Herod was forie for his rafh promiffe made to the woman dauncer, his daughter, when he heard her afke Saint Johns head, but kinge Henrie was nothinge at all forie for the promiffe he made of this holy Johns heade, but wilfully and malicioufly fought all vnlawfull meanes to cut it from the bodie, nether refpecting his age, [1] his vertue, his learninge, fanctitie of life, dignitie, nor other quallitie in his worthie perfonage. The fact of kinge Herod, for which Saint John dyed, did moft concerne the iniurie which Herod did to his brother, whofe wife he tooke. But the fact of kinge Henrie, wherfore our bleffed John dyed, did not only tuche the iniurie committed againft the vertuous ladie, his lawfull wife, but it contayned the expreffe contempt of our holy father the Pope, and of the authoritie of the Catholicke Church befides the occafion of finne and fcandall which it gave to the partie that did pretend title to her, whom the king would needes marrie. But what fhould I fpeake of Herode, whofe crueltie was nothinge to be compared to this kinge, for in malice which he fhewed to a great number of holy and learned men, principally to this, our holy father, he had neuer yet his like bearing the name of Chrift, and profeffing his faith. In vnthankfulnes he was much worfe then Alexander, for he did not only nothing confider the great affiaunce which his noble father, king Henrie the vij[th], had in this holy man, making him at his death one of his executors (as we haue before mentioned), nothing wayinge the finguler affeccion and creditt that his grandmother, that worthie ladie Margaret, Counteffe of Richmond [2] and Darbie, had in him above all the Prelats and bifhops of the land: but fetting at nought the great vertue, learninge, and holines which he perfectly knewe to be in him fo rare a bifhop, and vtterly

[1] Fol. 111, back.   [2] Fol. 112.

forgettinge the honor and fame which by him both he and all his realme had gotten, lyke a moſt vnthankfull prince, and moſt contemptuous of his foueraigne and holy father, the head of Chriſts church in earth, ſought out moſt wickedly all the meanes he coulde to intrappe this holy biſhop and vertuous Cardinall, and contrary both to the lawe of god and decrees of our holy mother, the Church, beinge a meere laie prince, and ſo havinge no authoritie nor iuriſdiccíon wherby he might lawfully thus proceed againſt an annointed biſhop *and* Cardinall of the Church of Rome, but that by entendinge the leaſt of the waies which he vſed againſt him, muſt of neceſſitie incurre the fore and greevous cenſure of excommunicacíon, accompanied with many other daungers and inconveniences more then can well be rehearſed. He (I ſaie), contemminge all theſe, did moſt wickedly take vpon him and vſurpe the authoritie which before his daies, neuer *Chriſt*en *and* Catholyke prince did, and (which John Calvin, an Heretick, did vtterly deteſt and condemne in him) againſt all law and reaſon moſt cruelly put to death this man of god, ouer whom, nether by law nor cuſtome he could haue any criminall iuriſdiccíon, but ought (yf he had made an offence) to have referred the hearing and diſcuſſing of his crime to his metropolitan, [1] or rather to the cheefe head of all biſhopps, to whom only the iudgment and hearinge of a biſhopps crime in a ſpirituall cauſe (as this was) doth and alwaies hath of right appertained. And as the enormities of king Henrie in this caſe were ſo exorbitant, and ſurpaſſing all lawe, reaſon, and conſcience, ſo is the wonderfull working of Almightie god (whoſe iudgments are ſecret and ſtrange in our ſights) much to be marked and noted in him and his adherents. for as god of his owne nature is patient and longe ſufferinge, becauſe he expecteth the amendment of our ſinfull lives, ſo is he alſo iuſt in his doings, and puniſheth greevouſly where no amendment is indevored, as now may well be perceived by theſe perſons that were perſecutors of this bleſſed man, for they eſcaped not the daunger of his heavie hand, as ſhall be declared vnto you.

And firſt, to begin with the ladie Ann Bullen as the cheef and principall cauſe for whom all this wofull tragedie begun, who was

[1] Fol. 112, back.

alſo cheef perſecutor of this holy man; marke how ſhe was in ſhort ſpace after caſte downe from the topp of her high honor and dignitie wherin ſhe was exalted, and for a moſt foule *and* abhominable inceſt committed with her owne brother, beſides ſundrie adultries with other perſons, was throwne into cruell and ſtrayte priſon, where ſhe remained not longe before ſhe was condemned to death by ſundrie noble men of this realme, that lately before were full plyable and readie to pleaſe her in all her co*mm*aundments, wherof ſome were [1]neere of kindred to her; yea, one of them her owne father: according to which condemnac*io*n ſhe was put to open and ſhamefull execution of death, leavinge behind her nothinge but an infamous name to continue for eu*er*. Of whoſe loſſe the kinge himſelf tooke ſo litle ſorrowe, that the verie next daie after ſhe was dead he was maryed to another wife.

Next that, the lord Crumwell is to be remembred, who with great dilligence ſolicited the matter to the kinge, and erneſtly provoked him in this and manie other ill purpoſes. He, beinge advaunced to ſuch honor and authoritie as no man in this realme at that time bare the lyke about the kinge, grewe at laſt into ſuch hatred amonge the noble men and co*mm*ons throughout the realme for his intollerable *and* tirannicall crueltie exerciſed ou*er* them, that finally he was by ſundrie practiſes brought alſo into the kings diſpleaſure, and ſo caſt into miſerable priſon, condemned to death by Acte of Parliament for hereſie and treaſon, and after executed accordinge to his iudgment, no man pittying his Caſe.

Then co*mm*eth to minde m*aiſte*r Thomas Cranm*er*, Archbiſhop of Canterburie, who of his owne powre without iuſt warrant or authoritie pronounced the ſentence of divorſe betwene the kinge and the queene, and.after callinge this holy man before him and others, caſt him into priſon with as much extremitie as could be ſhowed for refuſing the two new oathes, the one of the kings new marryage, the other of the Sup*r*emacie [2]from whence he was neu*er* deliu*er*ed till death ridd him of all worldly cares. This m*aiſte*r Cranmer, although he continewed his place and dignitie duringe the vnnaturall and cruell times of kinge Henrie and the infant his ſonne kinge Edward, yet at laſt in the

[1] Fol. 113.   [2] Fol. 113, back.

raigne of that moſt bleſſed ladie, Queene Marie, when the true light of iuſtice of Chriſts anncient and Catholicke religion began againe to ſhine, he was called to a reckonninge for many of his former ill doings, And laſtly, ſtanding ſtiffe in diuers horrible and fowle hereſies, was moſt worthily burnt with fire and conſumed to aſhes.

Lykewiſe m*aiſte*r Rich, the kings Solicitor, that gaue falſe teſtimonie againſt him, and was forſworne at his arraignement in ſo falſely betrayinge him, Although for manie yeres after he continewed corruptly gathering together of welth till the daies of king Henrie were ended, yet haue I bene credibly informed, that yf the kinge had lived but a few daies longer then he did, he was growne into ſuch diſpleaſure againſt him for ſundrie falſehoodes and deceipts, in fraudulent purchaſinge and exchangeinge of land between the kinge and him, wherein the kinge was deceaved of no ſmall valewe: And lykwiſe for diuers bribes extorted vpon manie of his ſubiects, that he was finally determined to have attainted him of fellonie, extorc*i*on, and periurie, and ſo in one howre to have ſpoyled him of all that great heape [1] which he ſo falſely had raked together in manie yeres before. But beinge after in the wicked time of the infants raigne advaunced to high honor and place far above his deſert, yet lived he to be depoſed againe of that place even by the ſame perſons that preferred him. But ſince in the daies of that noble and bleſſed queen marie of worthie memorie, he became penitent (as I have heard) for many of his offences; for the which god permitted him (as it may be thought) to die in better order then the reſt before did. But true it is that after his death his bodie eſcaped a narrow daunger of burninge: for at ſuch time as he was dead and his bodie laid into a Coffin, ceared and balmed, and certaine Candells ſet vpon the herſe, as the manner was; one of the Candells (ether by the will of god, or els by negligence of ſome of the watchers that were abſent) fell downe, and tooke houlde firſt of the Clothes and after of the Coffin, that in *th*e ende before any body was ware, the fire was faſtned vpon the cearecloathes, where this miſerable carcaſſe laye, and had without all doubt conſumed the ſame into aſhes, had it not then bene ſpeedily eſpied by certaine of *th*e ſervants by chaunce, who ſaved all for that time,

[1] Fol. 114.

though not without great daunger to the bodie, and the reſt of the howſe alſo. All which ſo narrowe eſcapes I can impute to nothinge but only to the goodnes of god, for that he conceived (as before is ſaid) ſome repentance, though I neuer heard of any pennance by him done at all.

[1] Laſte of all it is worthie to be remembred how iuſtly the kinge himſelf was plagued firſt by the inordinat number of his wives, beinge in all vj, and not one lawfull more then the firſt, as maie be thought. Of theſe vj two were repudiate, two beheaded for incontinencie, one killed wittingly in childbed for ſaveing of her childe, and the ſixt ſurvived him, wherin her fortune was better then the reſt of her fellowes: for (as I haue heard reported by ſuch as had no cauſe to lie) he was wearie of her longe before he dyed, and therfore yf he had lived but one yere longer, ment to have framed ſuch matter againſt her for hereſie, as ſhould haue coſt her her lyfe as it did ſome others of her predeſceſſors before. And as for heire male of his body which he ſo much deſired and made ſo great adooe for, as though the realme had bene vtterly vndone yf he had dyed without yſſue male, we ſee that god for ſome purpoſe permitted him at laſt to have a ſonne, rather (as it may be thought) that no ſillie women ſhould looſe their lives for ſatiſfying his licentious and vaine appetite, then for any other iuſt reſpect. But after his death the raigne of that ſonne was verie ſhort, and his yeres verie fewe ; ſo is there no great matter praiſe worthie to be written of him. But of things done vnder the color of his name and authoritie have we all great cauſe to lament, which [2] tended to nothinge els but the ouerthrowe and extirpacion of the Catholick faith here within this realme, as we felte and taſted, and ſhould ſtill have taſted daily more and more yf god had not taken him vpon ſome ſpeciall favour (as may be thought) and mercifull pittie which at laſt he began to have of this poore afflicted countrey, reduceinge it againe to the true and auncient faith, by the cutting awaie of ſuch an impe, at whoſe handes we were not to looke for more grace then the father by his pernitious examples had grafted in ſo inceſtious and damnable a ſtocke. Then note his vnmercifull and vnſpeakable crueltie, wherin he was once entred by the horrible

[1] Fol. 114, back. [2] Fol. 115.

murder of this holy prelate, he conceived fuch a bouldnes, and therwithall was ftroken with fuch a blindnes, *that* in crueltie he was to be accounted nothinge inferior to Nero, for whereas Nero committed execrable parricide in caufinge his naturall mother to be flaine, and not fatiate therwith commaundinge that in his prefence her bellie fhould be opened to the entent (as he faid) that vnnaturally he might beholde *the* place where he was conceived in her woumbe. This kinge Henrie, an other Nero, did not only perpetrate parricide and facriledge, but alfo that hainous treafon of Herefie all at one clappe, whiles in ryppinge the bowells of his mother, *the* holy Church and verie fpoufe of Chrift vpon earth, he labored to teare her in peeces, and difpifinge her authoritie (beinge but one of her rotten members) monftroufly tooke vpon him to be her fupreame heade; for this only acte (if he had done nothing els) alwais was and by law is accounted [1] fo enorme and exorbitant, that as he which withdraweth or detracteth from any peculier Church her right doth manifeft iniurie and wronge, fo he that goeth about to take awaie the priviledge of the Church of Rome, geven of *Chrift* himfelf, the fupreame heade of all Churches, falleth into herefie. And wheras the other tranfgreffor is to be termed iniurious and vnnaturall, this kind of offence in this is to be called both a fcifmaticke and an hereticke, for he doth violate faith and nature in attemptinge againft *the* church, which is the mother of faith. But this our fecond Nero was not yet content with this abhominable acte, but heaped a great many moe vpon it, rafinge to the ground holy monafteries, Priories, and all other forts of religious howfes, profaininge them with all *the* holie reliques and precious ornaments dedicate to the fervice of god, not fparing the bloodfhed of all fuch holy men and learned clerkes as preferred the pleafure of god and commandme*nt* of their mother the Catholick Church, before his vnlawfull lawes and wicked will. And for noble perfonages of this realme, both men and women, he fpared nether kindred nor other, yea, many times for a word fpeakinge he would revenge by death, were it fpoken vpon neu*er* fo reafonable a ground or caufe. By reafon wherof more of the nobillity were confumed in his daies, then in any three of his predifceffors fince this realme was firft

[1] Fol. 115, back.

inhabited, fo that in murder (yf it be well confidered) he paffed the cruell ¹Turke Selyn. To this ioyne his licentious and wanton expenfes wherby he confumed the treafure of his realme, and then fallinge into lacke turned his gould and filver into Copper, and after (fpendinge the fame vnthriftely) tooke of his fubiectes fo exceffively, that neuer prince in this realme lived with leffe love and favor of all good people, though amonge flatterers and parrafites (amonge whom this treafure was fpent) neuer any fo highly magnifyed and extolled. Then confider how iuftly he was plagued in his groffe bodie many yeres before his death, with foares and difeafes that grewe vpon him, by meane of drunken furfettes, idlenes, flouth, and vitious trade of life, amonge women, fparing nether kindred nor other yf fhe lyked his carnall appetite, wherby he became at laft fo impotent and loathfome, that when the Surgeants fhould dreffe him, it hath bene reported by fome of his privie chamber that they have fmelte the ill favour of his foares the fpace of two chambers before they came at him. Laftly and moft of all, waie the daunger of his miferable foul dyinge in the perilous ftate of excommunication without reconciliacion or repentance, knowne or heard of to the worlde; yea, it hath bene reported by fuch as were about him at his end that he dyed almoft in defperacion cryinge out vpon the phifitians becaufe they could not cure him, Sayinge, " have I thus rewarded you with livings and geven you fees, and none of you now able to helpe me when I have moft need of your helpe." And with that callinge for Sir Anthonie Dennye, an egregious flatterer about him, and comonly never farr from him, commaunded him to whipp them.

²And although he perceived at laft that by no meanes he could efcape death, yet what did he? Can any man report that in all the time of his ficknes he once called to god for mercie and forgevenes of his former wretched life: no truly. But fomtimes lying in a ftudie with himfelf, and fomtimes forrowinge as feemed by his countenance, would fodenly faie, " oh! I muft dye ": " yea, Sir," would fome or other faie fomtime, " you muft needs die once; fo muft I and euery man here, but I truft you fhall not die nowe." " Alas " (would he faie againe), " thinkeft thou that I fhall be faved when I die? for I have

¹ Fol. 116.   ² Fol. 116, back.

bene a kinge, and lived lyke a kinge." And no doubt, but even as
his life was finfull, fo after his death god fhewed a ftrange example
upon his wretched Carcaffe, for at fuch time as it was in preparinge to
be ceared and fpiced, by the Surgions in the chamber at weftminfter,
where he dyed, to be after removed downe to the Chappell, and fo
from thence to winfor, where it was buried; it chanced the faid
carcas by mifhap and ouer boifterous liftinge to fall to the ground,
out of which yffued fuch a quantitie of horrible and ftinking filthie
blood and matter, that it was no fmall trooble to a number about it
to clenfe the place againe, and to make readie againft the next daie
for the remove. But before all could be done there came into the
place (as I have bene credibly informed) a great black dogge, no man
could tell from whence, which dogge (while euery [1] bodie was occupied) filled himfelf fo full as his fides could hould with lycking vp
his filthie blood that was fpilte, and in the end efcaped without hurt
from the Garde and diuers others that ftrooke at him with their
halberts *and* other weapons, meaninge verily to have killed him yf
they coulde.

Others I could have named vnto you that were doers in this
bufines, and that of right great callinge, whom god worthily after
finifhed, fome by a fowle and fhamefull ende, fome by leavinge
them without yffue or kindred, wherby their landes and goodes after
their death came to the handes of ftraungers that fell in ftrife amonge
them felves, others were attainted, and therby not only their owne
bodies executed to fhamefull death, but alfo their landes and goods
beinge forfeited their children went a begginge. Some came to one
mifhap and fome to another, which yf it were written at large would
require a longe proceffe.

[2] Thefe beinge manifeft fignes and tokens of Godes indignacion and
heavie difpleafure againft this whole realme, for fo cruell and horrible
murderinge of his holy prophetts, it ftandeth vs in hand, and that
fpeedily without delay, to proftrate ourfelves before him, and with
humilitie to befeech him of his infinite mercie and goodnes, that we
be not accordinge to our defertes worthily punifhed, firft in this world,
by the intollerable yoke, and barbarous tyrannie of Infidells and Turkes

[1] Fol. 117.   [2] Fol. 118.   Part of Fol. 117 and all Fol. 117, back, is blank.

and after in the world to come by eue*r*laftinge paine and torment of hell fire. But that rather by the merritts and interceffion of this holy Martyr, this noble realme may once againe be reftored to that auncient and trewe *Chrif*tian faith in which our forefathers lived these thowfand yeres and more: And that we *the* dwellers therin and our pofteritie may once againe peaceably ferve him in the fame faith all the daies of our lives. And after in the world to come, glorifie him in his heavenly kingdome where he raigneth for ever and eue*r*. Amen.

FINIS.

The manufacturer's authorised representative in the EU for product safety is Oxford University Press España S.A. of El Parque Empresarial San Fernando de Henares, Avenida de Castilla, 2 - 28830 Madrid (www.oup.es/en or product.safety@oup.com). OUP España S.A. also acts as importer into Spain of products made by the manufacturer.
Printed and bound by CPI Group (UK) Ltd, Croydon, CR0 4YY

20/03/2026

02075337-0003